THEOLOGY IN ACTION

How the Rabbis of the Talmud Present Theology (Aggadah) in the Medium of the Law (Halakhah): An Anthology

Jacob Neusner

Studies in Judaism

University Press of America,® Inc.
Lanham · Boulder · New York · Toronto · Oxford

Copyright © 2006 by
University Press of America,® Inc.
4501 Forbes Boulevard
Suite 200
Lanham, Maryland 20706
UPA Acquisitions Department (301) 459-3366

PO Box 317
Oxford
OX2 9RU, UK

All rights reserved
Printed in the United States of America
British Library Cataloging in Publication Information Available

Library of Congress Control Number: 2006923921
ISBN-13: 978-0-7618-3488-5 (paperback : alk. paper)
ISBN-10: 0-7618-3488-5 (paperback : alk. paper)

∞™ The paper used in this publication meets the minimum
requirements of American National Standard for Information
Sciences—Permanence of Paper for Printed Library Materials,
ANSI Z39.48—1984

Studies in Judaism

EDITOR

Jacob Neusner
Bard College

EDITORIAL BOARD

Alan J. Avery-Peck
College of the Holy Cross

Herbert Basser
Queens University

Bruce D. Chilton
Bard College

José Faur
Bar Ilan University

William Scott Green
University of Rochester

Mayer Gruber
Ben-Gurion University of the Negev

Günter Stemberger
University of Vienna

James F. Strange
University of South Florida

Contents

PREFACE vii

1. INTRODUCTION 1

   i. Talmud-Study in Judaism 2
   ii. Halakhah and Aggadah in the Bavli's Cogent Statement 3
   iii. The Centrality of Reasoned Disputes 4
   iv. The Talmud's Two Languages 6
   v. Translating the Bavli 7
   vi. Reconstructing Thought. Special Problems in Translating the Talmud 7
   vii. An Analytical Translation and Commentary Effected through Semiotics 9
   viii. An Analytical Reference System 10

2. THE TALMUD'S THEOLOGICAL FRAMEWORK 13

   i. Theology in Narrative-Exegetical Form: The Gemara's Other Component 13
   ii. How the Halakhah and the Aggadah Cohere in Theology 14
   iii. The Monotheist System of Rabbinic Judaism: The Main Components and how They Cohere 15
   iv. The Aggadic Dimension: Adam and Israel in the World. Genesis Rabbah XIX:IX.1-2 17
   v. The Halakhic Dimension: Israel at Home 21
   vi. How the Halakhah Realizes the Aggadah: The Case of the Halakhah of the Fruit of a Tree in the First Three Years after it is planted, tractate 'Orlah. Sifra CCII.I.1 22
   vii. The Halakhic Realization of the Aggadic Theology Seen Whole: Actualizing the Torah's Story 26

3. THE TALMUD'S UNION OF HALAKHAH AND AGGADAH: THE HALAKHAH OF GENTILE IDOLATRY AND THE AGGADAH OF GENTILE REJECTION OF THE TORAH 37

   i. Israel and the Nations 37
   ii. Bavli Abodah Zarah 1:1 I.1-33/2a-5b 39
   iii. From the Mishnah to the Talmud, from the Halakhah to the Aggadah 59
   iv. Theology in the Context of the Law. Bavli Abodah Zarah 3:8A-C II.1-2/48b. Pesiqta deRab Kahana XXVIII:I.1 61

4. THE TALMUD'S UNION OF HALAKHAH AND AGGADAH: THE HALAKHAH OF SELF-DENIAL ON THE DAY OF ATONEMENT AND THE AGGADAH OF REPENTANCE 67

    i. Rite and Right. The Fathers According to Rabbi Nathan IV:V.2 67
    ii. Bavli Yoma Chapter Eight: An Overview 70
    iii. The Halakhah of Atonement and the Aggadah of Repentance. Bavli Yoma 8:9 III.3-VI.5/86a-87b 84
    iv. Prophetic Theology in the Context of the Law: The Priority of the Right Attitude 94

5. THE TALMUD'S UNION OF HALAKHAH AND AGGADAH: THE HALAKHAH OF CRIMINAL JUSTICE AND THE AGGADAH OF THE RESURRECTION OF THE DEAD 99

    i. Criminal Justice, Death and Resurrection. Mishnah-tractate Sanhedrin 6:2, 5, Bavli Sanhedrin 4:5 VI.1/39b 99
    ii. Bavli Sanhedrin: An Overview of the Halakhah 105
    iii. Bavli Sanhedrin: An Overview of the Aggadah. The Exposition of the Statement, "All Israel has a portion in the world to come." 111
    iv. The Aggadah of Sanhedrin: The Mishnah's Provision of Resurrection and Who is Excluded. Mishnah-tractate Sanhedrin Chapter Eleven, Bavli Sanhedrin 11:1/I.2-14/90b-91b 129
    v. How the Talmud Finds in Scripture the Foundations for the Doctrine of Resurrection.. Bavli Sanhedrin 11:1 I.27ff./91bff 133
    vi. The Outcome of the Union of Halakhah and Aggadah 140

6. EPILOGUE: DEFINING JUDAISM. THE OTHER SIDE OF REASON: LET GOD BE GOD 143

    i. Defining Judaism, Explaining History. Bavli Makkot 3:15-16 II.1/23b-24a, Bavli Makkot 3:15-16 II.4/24a-b 143
    ii. Let God be God. Bavli Menahot 3:7 II.5/29B 147

FOR FURTHER REFERENCE 149

Preface

While in contemporary culture we tend to resort to a single, if broadly-defined, range of discourse to set down the results of systematic thought about public matters of the social order, in Rabbinic Judaism that is not the case. Two media serve for that purpose, two modes of writing about two distinct topics, law and lore. The authoritative documents of that Judaism set forth the entire structure of belief and system of behavior in two distinct modes of discourse, Halakhic and Aggadic, that is to say, statements of law, statements of lore, broadly construed. In this anthology I show how the Talmud of Babylonia, a.k.a., the Bavli, sets forth in a dual discourse the single, coherent theology of Rabbinic Judaism in its account of normative action.

In the Bavli the Halakhah serves in the setting forth norms of behavior (action, practice, subject to social sanctions in this world and age), Aggadah, norms of belief (attitude, emotion, conviction, subject to supernatural sanctions in Heaven and in the world to come). Viewed as ideal types, the Halakhah defines the norm, setting forth what is obligatory, the Aggadah, specifies what exceeds the norm and goes beyond the measure of the law. The one portrays the ordinary, the other, the extraordinary. The distinction between the two types of knowledge carries over into the two types of writing that convey the knowledge, and the two categorizations of discourse, Halakhah and Aggadah, is native to the texts of Rabbinic Judaism. Each is readily identified; a Halakhic composition can never be confused with an Aggadic one, formal traits and intellectual characteristics always differentiating the one from the other. These represent, then, native categories of the Rabbinic literature and its religious system. What makes the Bavli special is its presentation of both genres of thought and writing, and here we see examples of how they work side by side in unity to define the norms of theology and translate those norms into rules of correct conduct.

The striking differences of style and substance that differentiate the two categories of discourse present the question of how they intersect in a single coherent statement, a system that holds together its two distinct media of thought and expression. The Bavli alone answers that question. It is where the two intersect, and that leads to the question: how do Aggadah and Halakhah constitute a coherent religious structure and make in common a single systemic statement? There can be no doubt whatsoever that the Halakhah and the Aggadah in the canonical documents of formative Rabbinic Judaism form a cogent whole, each carrying out its distinctive task. But precisely where, within the formative literature of Normative Judaism, they join together, what affect the one exercises upon the other, and how the whole — the Bavli's systematic statement of Rabbinic Judaism — exceeds and transcends the sum of the parts — the Halakhah, the Aggadah — remains to be seen.

I owe thanks for much valuable advice to Professor William S. Green, University of Rochester. I consulted Professor Herbert Basser at a number of points and appreciate his counsel. I received much appreciated advice from Professors Stefan C. Reif, Cambridge University, Richard Kalmin, Jewish Theological Seminary of America. Robert Brody, Hebrew University of Jerusalem, and Rabbi Avi Shafrin, Agudath Israel. My cordial thanks to all.

Jacob Neusner
Institute of Advanced Theology
Bard College
Annandale-on-Hudson, NY 12504

06/01/04

1

Introduction

"In the beginning God created [heaven and earth]" (Gen. 1:1):

In the cited verse the Torah speaks, "I was the work-plan of the Holy One, blessed be he."

In the accepted practice of the world, when a mortal king builds a palace, he does not build it out of his own head, but he follows a work-plan.

Thus the Holy One, blessed be he, consulted the Torah when he created the world.

GENESIS RABBAH I:I.2

In theological terms the Talmud records the oral part of the instruction or tradition revealed by God to Moses at Sinai. In secular terms the Talmud of Babylonia, a.k.a., the Bavli, is a law code and a commentary, complemented by topical expositions on theological and Scriptural themes. The code is the Mishnah, a philosophical law code that reached closure in the Land of Israel in ca. 200 C.E. The commentary is the Gemara, a systematic reading of four of the six divisions of the Mishnah, those that deal with holy time, family life, the civil order, and the conduct of the (then-destroyed) Temple and its sacrificial offerings and support therefor. Omitted are the first division of the Mishnah, on agriculture, and the sixth division, on purities. Concluded in ca. 600 C.E. in Babylonia, then a province of the Iranian Empire under the Sasanian dynasty, the Talmud is important because it defines the law and theology of normative Judaism.

In Judaic theological terms the Talmud is a holy book and studying it forms an act of piety. That is because the Talmud participates in the process of the revelation and transmission of the Torah, or Instruction, revealed by God to Moses at Sinai, and handed on in writing and in oral tradition. In point of fact, the Bavli forms the climax and conclusion of the formative age of Judaism because it joins law to theology, exposition to exegesis, in a massive, coherent, authoritative statement.

To explain: the Rabbinic sages in their authoritative commentary to the book of Genesis, Genesis Rabbah, ca. 450 C.E., cited above, read the opening line of Genesis to say that God looked into the Torah and created the world. Consequently, the Torah given by God to Moses at Sinai affords access to God's plan for the creation of the world. It records what and how God thinks, God's rationality. That conception of the Torah is where the Talmud enters into the story. The Talmud in its analysis of the Torah's revealed law and theology deciphers the Torah's plan. It does so by making concrete the processes of applied reason and practical logic that are realized in the Torah and that guided creation. Working back from detail to the governing principles of thought, the Talmud's representation of the Torah reveals the working and the results of God's reason.

I. TALMUD-STUDY IN JUDAISM

When the faithful of Judaism study the Talmud, therefore, they do more than open a text to acquire facts of law and theology or to solve exegetical problems of Scripture. They encounter God in intellect, mind meeting mind, in company with every generation of sages and disciples. The meeting commences when the Talmud actively analyzes and systematizes those facts, asks questions about them, explores their implications. The Talmud then articulates the logic that animates the givens of the law and of theology. It uncovers the plan God adopted in making the world. That is how, in line with the approach of the Rabbinic exegetes to Genesis 1:1, the Talmud's representation of the Torah, written and oral, affords a glimpse into the mind of God.

Participating in the Talmud's open-ended contention and joining its argument about revealed truth affords the faithful access to God as God is made manifest in the Torah. It follows that for Judaism studying the Talmud constitutes an act of piety. But it is a form of religious encounter particular to Judaism. The Talmud, though represented as the writing down of the oral tradition of the Torah of Sinai, is not comparable, in Judaism, to the Bible in Christianity. It plays no role in the liturgy of synagogue worship. It is not so easily accessible to the faithful as are the narratives and prophecies and parables of Scripture. Although for Judaism the Talmud, like the Bible for Christianity, does transmit God's revelation, it does so in its own way.

These claims of the Talmud's importance and exemplary interest define the task of this reader. It is to show principal propositions. I set forth what the Talmud says in theology expressed in the context of law. This is an anthology, and I provide long abstracts of the Talmud, together with systematic outlines of important expositions. That is how I propose not only to describe from the outside, but to

1. Introduction

render accessible from the inside, what is represented by the Rabbinic sages as the particular encounter of humanity's mind with God's mind in the Torah as mediated by the Talmud. These abstracts and expositions through outlines are chosen to make accessible the reader's direct encounter with the document, so far as that is possible in translation.

The reader faces a daunting task, because following Talmudic analysis and argument demands concentration. Seeing the cogency of sequences of topical expositions is not always easy. While all is logical and orderly, therefore accessible, much is also dense and elliptical. The writing of the Talmud cannot be called lapidary. And much is taken for granted but not spelled out. A translation can accomplish just so much. The mode of Talmudic discourse has few counterparts in the world of general culture addressed in these pages, The legal and theological topics that are investigated, moreover, do not emerge from everyday transactions. Modes of thought are unfamiliar. We do not ordinarily ask law to yield theology, or theology to emerge from concrete social norms. But that is what the Talmud requires of those that would witness, and even join, its on-going conversation.

Few writings, religious or secular, accord to humanity a higher compliment than does the Talmud. This tribute it pays in its premise that humanity's mind and God's mind correspond, so that humanity can understand the Torah. Every page of the Talmud affirms that when the Torah says that humanity is created by God "in our image, after our likeness" (Genesis 1:26), it means that humanity is able to comprehend as God comprehends, so in some ways to think like God and therefore understand the Torah. In secular language it is as though we all were philosophers and mathematicians — a high compliment indeed.

II. Halakhah and Aggadah in the Bavli's Cogent Statement

Of what kind of writing, exactly, is the Talmud composed? The Gemara in fact is comprised by two distinct sorts of writing, each particular to its subject matter, both bearing distinctive media of form and of logical analysis. The one is the law, in Hebrew: Halakhah. The other is theology in narrative form, in Hebrew: Aggadah. The Halakhic passages are focused on the Mishnah but always in close concert with Scripture. The Aggadic passages focus on Scripture, establishing its meaning and finding its implications. The exposition here attends to the Aggadah in the context of the Halakhah, showing how the law and theology join together to make a single coherent statement of the Torah. We shall see how the Gemara's principal work was to unite into a coherent statement the two components of the Torah, Scripture and its theology, the Mishnah and its law.

How did the work of reconstruction take place? The Rabbinic sages in the Talmud responded to Scripture and the Mishnah by dismantling the narrative of the former (Scripture) and the topical exposition of the latter (the Mishnah). These were reduced to sense-units, clauses and sentences, bits and pieces. The authors of compositions and compilers of composites of compositions of which the Gemara is comprised then recast the parts into a whole of their own design. They did two things. First, they systematized the law in such a way as to expose its inner ontology. Second, developing Scripture's own media and matching the character and requirements of its data, they through narrative ordered and highlighted exemplary points of the theology they deemed to animate the entire structure. And at critical points they joined the Aggadah to the Halakhah, the theological-exegetical exposition of Scripture to the legal account of the Mishnah. The Gemara brought the two together, the only systematic union of the two kinds of writing in Rabbinic antiquity, and rare afterward.[1] What emerged was a system of remarkable cogency, joining norms of deed to those of deliberation, action and attitude. That work of uniting Halakhah and Aggadah constitutes the Gemara's most remarkable achievement.

III. THE CENTRALITY OF REASONED DISPUTES

But that substantive, theological accomplishment should not obscure a formal achievement that defined the character of the writing. That is the preservation, for future generations' participation, of dispute, debate, contention and conflict. Readers of the Mishnah and the Gemara will rapidly notice its single most striking trait, the ubiquitous dispute. That comes to expression in the sages' invention of a literary form for preserving disagreements: *statement of an issue, X says... Y says...* and variations. That form — characteristic of, and unique, to Rabbinic Judaism among the Judaic cultures — moves from the Mishnah and the Tosefta through the Talmud of the Land of Israel and the collections of Scriptural commentary of late antiquity and reaches its climax in the dialectical argument unique to the Talmud of Babylonia.

Schism expressed through disputes — not merely implicit inconsistency in viewpoint but articulated statements of disagreement or alternative choices of interpreting a common text — dominate and lend energy to the Gemara's discourse. But disputes and alternative interpretations of a common datum form a medium of expressing coherence. Conflicts between named Rabbinic authorities underscore the prevailing consensus about fundamental truth. Indicators of concurrence in deep structures of thought, for instance, common denominators among successive readings of a single problem, properly situated in perspective, abound.

Neither kind of composition in the Talmud, the Halakhic or the Aggadic fears difference of opinion. Both derive strength from it. That attitude of mind derives from the logic of theological conviction: it is the trait of the Torah, properly, reverently received in the reasoned manner in which God gives the Torah. Marking the outer bounds of schism underscores the deep layers of concurrence on the law. Highlighting how different views in fact cohere likewise uncovers the profound cogency, the systematic character, of the theology and ethics that come to the surface

1. Introduction

in the particularity and variety of exegesis. That is because the exclusive Halakhic ruling and the inclusive Aggadic composite concur on the coherence of the teachings of the Torah as set forth by the Rabbinic sages.

Disputes about the law ground matters in a thoroughly examined foundation of reason. Mere authority matters less than applied reasoning and practical logic, which refine the law through thorough contention. That is the point of the following narrative about the ubiquitous conflict in law between Yohanan and his disciple, Simeon b. Laqish, who was to begin with a thief but was redeemed and educated in Torah-study by Yohanan. I present the Aramaic parts in italics, the Hebrew parts in plain type; the shift in languages is explained in a moment.

BAVLI BABA MESIA 7:1 I.12/84A

A. *One day there was a dispute in the school house [on the following matter]:* As to a sword, knife, dagger, spear, hand-saw, and scythe — at what point in making them do they become susceptible to become unclean? It is when the process of manufacturing them has been completed [at which point they are deemed useful and therefore susceptible]. And when is the process of manufacturing them completed?

B. R. Yohanan said, "When one has tempered them in the crucible."

C. R. Simeon b. Laqish said, "When one has furbished them in water."

D. *[R. Yohanan] said to him, "Never con a con-man" [lit.: a robber is an expert at robbery].*

E. *He said to him, "So what good did you ever do for me? When I was a robber, people called me, 'my lord' [lit.: rabbi], and now people call me 'my lord.'"*

F. *He said to him, "I'll tell you what good I've done for you, I brought you under the wings of the Presence of God."*

G. *R. Yohanan was offended, and R. Simeon b. Laqish fell ill. His [Yohanan's] sister [Simeon b. Laqish's wife] came to him weeping, saying to him, "[Heal my husband,] do it for my children's sake!"*

H. He said to her, "'Leave your fatherless children. I will preserve them alive' (Jer. 49:11)."

I. "Then do it on account of my widowhood!"

J. He said to her, "'...and let your widows trust in me' (Jer. 49:11)." [He gave her no satisfaction and made no promises.]

K. *R. Simeon b. Laqish died, and R. Yohanan was much distressed afterward. Rabbis said, "Who will go and restore his spirits? Let R. Eleazar b. Pedat go, because his traditions are well-honed."*

L. *He went and took a seat before him. At every statement that R. Yohanan made, he comments, "There is a Tannaite teaching that sustains your view."*

M. *He said to him, "Are you like the son of Laqisha? When I would state something, the son of Laqisha would raise questions against my position on twenty-four grounds, and I would find twenty-four solutions, and it naturally followed that the tradition was broadened, but you say to me merely, 'There is a Tannaite teaching that sustains your view.' Don't I know that what I say is sound?"*

N. *So he went on tearing his clothes and weeping, "Where are you, the son of Laqisha, where are you, the son of Laqisha," and he cried until his mind turned from him. Rabbis asked mercy for him, and he died.*

For our purpose the principal entry is M: essential to the process of presenting and analyzing the law is the discipline of reasoned contention. And that is what the Gemara contributes in its reading of Scripture and the Mishnah, Aggadah and Halakhah.

IV. THE TALMUD'S TWO LANGUAGES

The passage cited just now shows that the Babylonian Talmud is a bilingual document. When it came to citations from prior, non-scriptural authorities, the Rabbinic sages used one formation of the Hebrew language, specifically, Middle, or Mishnaic, Hebrew; when it came to the conduct of their own analytical process, the Talmud's authorities used one dialect of the Aramaic language, Eastern or Talmudic Aramaic. The Mishnah, source of authoritative law, and correlative legal traditions are always cited in Mishnaic Hebrew. The Gemara's analytical passages are in Aramaic, its expositions of traditions, ordinarily in Hebrew. As a rule of thumb, therefore, for the Talmud's Halakhic discourse, Hebrew serves as the medium of authoritative traditions, Aramaic as the medium of analysis and criticism.

In point of fact, the Talmud is in one language, not two, and that language is Aramaic. The infrastructure of the document, its entire repertoire of editorial conventions and sigla, are in Aramaic. When a saying is assigned to a named authority, the saying may be in Hebrew or in Aramaic, and the same named authority may be given sayings in both languages — even within the same sentence. But the editorial and conceptual infrastructure of the document comes to expression only in Aramaic, and when no name is attached to a statement, that statement is always in Aramaic, unless it forms part of a larger, autonomous Hebrew composition, cited by, or parachuted down into, "the Talmud."

The choice of one language over the other marked what was said as one type of statement rather than another. If, therefore, we know which language is used, we also know where we stand in the expression of thought, and the very language in which a statement is made therefore forms part of the method of thought and even the message of discourse of the document. My translation devises visual signals to take account of the bi-lingualism of the writing, as I shall now explain.

1. Introduction

V. TRANSLATING THE BAVLI

This brings us to the problem of translating the Bavli and the choices I have made in my translation. Abstract observations on issues of law and theology, context and coherence, do not prepare the reader for the actualities of the Talmud. Nothing that merely describes the document could do so. The Mishnah and Gemara do not yield their meanings casually. When transferred literally, word for word, into another language than its own, the Gemara produces gibberish. The Gemara everywhere presupposes knowledge it does not supply, the working of verbal symbols that convey meanings it does not define. Without a sizable corpus of signals and amplifying language, afforded by commentaries or by translations or, ideally, by a living sage in the chain of tradition from Sinai, whom the student serves as a disciple, the whole is simply inaccessible.

Translating the Talmud presents problems common to all texts deriving from another time and place and also some that are particular to this document.[2] Everyone understands that meanings do not emerge merely through rendering what one language says in words that in our language approximate the original. It is a commonplace that a translation always constitutes a commentary and requires a process of cultural mediation. The task is not merely to find words in English that render the sense of words in Hebrew and Aramaic. It is to transfer patterns of thought and sensibility from one cultural context to another, and that always involves the exercise of taste and judgment. That is so for all translations from language to language: the requirement to translate cultures, which by definition do not match, whether by category-formation or by conceptual building blocks, but only approximate one another. Some documents sustain close to a literal rendition, so that from the English we can reconstruct the Hebrew. The Mishnah is one such document, self-contained in its syntax and coherent in its exposition, so that a nearly-literal translation produces, if not elegant English, then in any event a statement that is intelligible. The same is so of the Tosefta and of the free-floating Halakhic compositions that are assigned to the Mishnah's authorities and that are preserved in the Talmud.

VI. RECONSTRUCTING THOUGHT. SPECIAL PROBLEMS IN TRANSLATING THE TALMUD

But the Gemara is not that way, and that brings us to the special problems connected with rendering the document accessible beyond its own cultural and linguistic boundaries. The Gemara does not transcribe fully-exposed thought. It is made up in the main of notes that make possible the reconstruction of discourse. But the translation (or appended commentary) must supply massive blocks of interpolated explanation to make the notes work. The translator becomes part of the process of not recapitulation but the sheer reconstruction of thought-processes and their outcome. Translating poetry — best attempted by poets, who combine profound learning and intuition — presents no more intractable problems for Greek and Latin than translating thoughts scarcely articulated in the original Hebrew and Aramaic does for the Gemara. The problem derives not from philology or from text-criticism,[3] though both contribute to a careful portrait of the document. It emerges from the very intellectual quality of the document, not its obscurity but its profundity and its premises concerning the context in which it is received, to which it directs its address.

And that introduces a peculiarity common to ancient texts that imposes a still weightier burden on the translator-expositor of the Talmud: the occasional disorganization of discourse and its technical causes. To understand the problem, we begin with the practices of today. When I am composing an essay or a sustained exposition, I aim at a coherent, flowing, continuous exposition of ideas, in which each sentence is logically continuous with the one before and connected to the one following. Therefore I subordinate, in footnotes, bits and pieces of clarification, e.g., facts, meanings of words and phrases, that readers will find useful, but that will greatly impede the exposition if left in the body of the text. So in the text I make my main point, and in footnotes I add supplementary information, even further thoughts. Not only so, but when I am writing a book, I may wish to take up an entire subject and present it in a systematic way, but I may also find that the proposition that is subject to exposition at a given point does not allow for the systematic exposition of an important topic. Or I may wish to clarify a detail, interpolate a thought, enrich my presentation without corrupting its coherence. Now what do I do? I simply write up the clarifying remark and make it a footnote, or the topical exposition and place it into an appendix. In that way readers benefit from the information, but the progress of exposition flows unimpeded. In a collective document, drawing on bits and pieces of completed compositions and forming of the whole a coherent composite, the inclusion of odds and ends is both essential and confusing.

But that is not how matters play out in the Talmud. Its compilers and compositors insert bits of information and fragments of thought without securing continuity of thought and argument. Everything is mixed together in the main body of the text, the main point, glosses and interpolations all in succession. Asides break up the flow of exposition and argument, and footnotes, interpolations, and excurses follow one after another, so the readers have to keep track of the main point and what is subordinate to that point and create an outline on their own to yield intelligible thought. That is because the writers of the Talmud, wanting to include clarification and asides of various kinds,[4] had no alternative. The technology of footnotes and appendices and the similar media by which writers in our own place and time protect the cogency of their presentation are the gift of movable type and printing (not to mention, in this glorious age, the miracle of the computer and word-processing. Since the Rabbinic sages (like everyone else in antiquity)

1. Introduction

had to put everything together in interminable columns of undifferentiated words, without punctuation, without paragraphing, without signals of what is primary and what is secondary, what we have demands a labor of differentiation.

VII. AN ANALYTICAL TRANSLATION AND COMMENTARY EFFECTED THROUGH SEMIOTICS

Until now none of the Talmud's many translations, complete or partial, from Middle Hebrew and Eastern Aramaic into German, Russian, Israeli Hebrew, and as many as a dozen [!] into British or American English, has signaled the components of the document or shown the place of the parts in the unfolding and systematic exposition that is underway. My translation solves that problem by giving various signals as to the character and position of each declarative sentence in a given composition. These signals begin with a clear indication of the main proposition and purpose of a given composition, then graphically mark out secondary developments, interpolations, appended topical excurses, and the like. Semiotic markings are executed mainly through graphics made possible by the computer; I signal my views on the place and role of every unit of thought by a simple medium of spatial organization and variation that, before computers would have been exceedingly difficult to execute, but, more likely, beyond my imagination. This I do in a variety of ways.

First, since the Gemara forms a commentary to the Mishnah (and correlative sources, which need not detain us), I distinguish the Mishnah from the Gemara by placing the Mishnah (and correlative sources, the Tosefta for example) in bold face type, the Gemara in plain type.

Second, once the Mishnah has been cited, the Gemara will ordinarily follow a program of citation and gloss. Each thought-unit in the Gemara's composite devoted to a given Mishnah composition forms the equivalent of a paragraph. I differentiate the paragraphs, giving each its own numeral (of which more in a moment).

Third, the secondary expansions inserted within an exposition are marked off via indentation at the left hand margin. What carries forward the analytical process is flush with the margin. Then the bits and pieces of information and gloss that we should likely place n footnotes, the entire apparatus of amplification by which the Mishnah-commentary supplied by the Gemara is comprised are separated out through a process of indentation. Where an interpolation interrupts an exposition, I indent the left margin of the interpolation, and restore that margin when the discussion resumes. Where an interpolation itself bears a gloss, I further indent the gloss. Sometimes to portray the construction of a composite and the interplay of bits and pieces within it, I have to indent four or five times. So the spatial signals form a commentary on my part that forms judgments on what is primary and continuous and what is secondary and interpolated.

Fourth, there is the matter of the bi-lingual character of the Gemara, in Hebrew and in Aramaic. Since, as just noted, the shift from language to language marks a shift of the character of discourse, from expository to analytical. I show the reader where the shift takes place. This is done by using italics for Aramaic, plain type for Hebrew.

Fifth, the identification of "sentences," completed units of thought, itself demands attention. What the Talmud lacked until my translation was a reference system. A passage would be cited by page number, with obverse or reverse side indicated, thus Bavli Berakhot 2a — a sizable discussion — would have to serve for all the sentences on that page. Sometimes we are given, "page 2a toward the bottom" — not a precise marker. While citing the received marking system, in addition I mark each unit of thought (sentence, ordinarily) with a letter, each composition of such units of thought (paragraph, in general) into a complete proposition with an Arabic numeral, and each composite of propositions that forms a completed exposition by a Roman number, with a clear statement of the topic or proposition of the whole. All of this is in the sequence marked at the head by a Mishnah-paragraph.

VIII. AN ANALYTICAL REFERENCE SYSTEM

Thus Mishnah-tractate X 3:1 I.1.A signals [1] Mishnah Tractate X [2] Chapter Three, [3] Paragraph One of the Mishnah-tractate chapter, [4] unit I of the Gemara's exposition of that Mishnah-paragraph, [5] paragraph 1 of that unit, [6] sentence A of that paragraph — and so throughout. I also record the received system, e.g., 2a-5b means Talmud page 2, obverse side of the page, through page 5, reverse side of the page. Until my translation was completed, there was no detailed reference system for the Talmud (or any other document of formative Rabbinic Judaism). That detailed reference system made possible a complete outline of both Talmuds and all the other classical documents, which I have also translated. The outline then shows how the Bavli forms a coherent, carefully constructed, cogent document.

The whole therefore yields a visual portrait of the discourse of the Talmud. These traits of that visual portrait, reproduced in the abstracts that make up the shank of this book, form the foundation of my translations, because they define the units of coherent discourse and place them into the context of the exposition of the Mishnah-paragraph under discussion. They call to the reader's attention the traits of structure that predominate, consistently, throughout the thirty-seven tractates of the Talmud.

When we speak of "structure," we begin with a clear account of what is primary to a sustained discussion and what is secondary, and how the whole holds together. As I said, I indent what is secondary, and further indent what is tertiary and so forth. By these visual signals, I make possible the immediate recognition of the traits of the writing, seen both whole and in its component parts. It then becomes

1. Introduction

simple to outline the Talmud, from the Mishnah-paragraph at the head, through the components of the attached Gemara.

In addition, I have prepared a complete outline of the Talmud's thirty-seven tractates,[5] showing how the Mishnah provides the main lines of exposition, the Gemara secondary and tertiary expositions of subsidiary points of clarification or analysis, with interpolated units of information to complement the whole. The possibility of executing such an outline leaves no doubt that we deal with a focused, coherent and well-constructed document. In the shank of the book, I utilize that outline to present an account of the Gemara's exposition of large ideas.

ENDNOTES

[1] The other work of theological synthesis and Halakhic analysis yielding a systematic statement is that of Moses Maimonides in his Guide to the Perplexed and Mishneh Torah, respectively. But Maimonides kept the two separate, not making a coherent statement of the two in one place. That remarkable achievement remained unique to the Talmud.

[2] I omit reference to a commonplace problem facing all translators of all ancient texts, the absence of punctuation. The documents lack paragraphing, footnotes and appendices and other aids to the reader's comprehension of matters. That trait of the manuscripts spills over into the printed texts. The earliest printed editions simply copied the extant manuscripts (of which, for the Talmud, there is only one complete manuscript), and even now, the classical published texts of the Talmud omit most punctuation and marks of paragraphing. The division of the undifferentiated lines of type into distinct sentences, paragraphs, and the like must be accomplished by the translator. More often than not, deciding where a sentence begins and ends forms part of the translator's commentary.

[3] We have no critical text for the entire Talmud of Babylonia, only for some tractates. Collections of variant manuscript readings, compiled by computer, contain no judgments of meaning and intent. I translate the standard printed text, following the principal commentaries and using the available dictionaries, checking my work constantly against that of the British translation published by Soncino Press (London, 1948, in a complete printing).

[4] That we confront an editorial decision to include extraneous opinion and information to present a comprehensive formulation of matters is shown in a simple way. Other Rabbinic documents, besides the Talmud of Babylonia, do not tolerate the mixture of exposition, interpolation, and gloss in a single composition, but produce coherent and continuous exposition of ideas. A comparison of the Mishnah, which does yield coherent discourse, with the Gemara, which does not, shows that the meandering and disorganized presentation of the Talmud is characteristic of the Talmud and not of all Rabbinic texts of the formative age.

[5] *The Talmud of Babylonia. A Complete Outline.* Atlanta, 1995-6: Scholars Press for *USF Academic Commentary Series.* Now: Lanham, MD. University Press of America, in four volumes, eight parts. I did the same for the Talmud of the Land of Israel and then presented the two Talmuds' outlines side by side for systematic comparison and contrast, but these have no bearing upon the task of this book.

2

The Talmud's Theological Framework

I. THEOLOGY IN NARRATIVE-EXEGETICAL FORM: THE GEMARA'S OTHER COMPONENT

The Talmud reaches its apex when it presents theology, Aggadah, in the context of law, Halakhah. That union of spirit and form is unique in the Rabbinic setting. The Rabbinic documents devoted to scriptural exegesis and theology[1] contain very little exposition of law. The documents of the Halakhah, from the Mishnah forward, introduce Aggadic writing very sparingly indeed. Completed before the advent of the Talmud of Babylonia, the Halakhic compilations from the Mishnah forward — the Tosefta, the Talmud of the Land of Israel, and the Baraita-corpus — devoted slight attention to Aggadic narrative or to theological issues.

Faced with the separation of law from theology and theology from law, the Talmud's compilers changed the picture completely. They encompassed in their composites not only systematic Halakhic exposition but equally well-articulated Aggadic discussion. The compilers thus correlated Aggadic compositions with the Halakhic setting in which they are introduced, each shedding light on the other. In significant measure, therefore, they integrated the Aggadic exposition of theology, narrative, and wisdom with the Halakhic presentation of topics of the law. It was the Talmud's success in joining the law and theology, Halakhah and the Aggadah in a single coherent document that made it the summa of Judaism: the design of a social order that realized God's design for humanity.

Approximately 60% of the Gemara in volume is devoted to the three components of the Talmud's Halakhic discourse that we have now surveyed: [1] Mishnah-exegesis (illustrated in Chapter One), [2] amplification of the law of the Mishnah (shown in Chapter Two), and [3] debates and dialectical inquiry into the Halakhah (introduced in Chapter Three). That leaves about 40%, more in some tractates less in others, for theological topics and the exposition of Scripture's narrative, prophecy, and exhortation.[2] The contrast between the two Talmuds —

the one of the Land of Israel, closed in ca. 400, the other of Babylonia two hundred years later — tells the story. Approximately 90% of the first Talmud's units of discourse in my sample probe of five tractates of the Talmud of the Land of Israel deal with the Mishnah, doing so in the Mishnah's terms and framework. Scarcely 10% of my sample addresses Aggadic matters — a perfunctory glance in the direction of theology.

The Talmud of Babylonia pioneered in another aspect as well. The same intellectual rigor brought by the Talmudic sages to the encounter with the Mishnah characterized their thought-processes when they turned to Scripture. Only the subjects change from issues of normative conduct to those of normative conviction, from action to attitude, from behavior to belief, always in dialogue with Scripture.

Unsurprisingly, with the movement from Halakhic to Aggadic discourse the literary media shift as well. Aggadic compositions are of two types. First come appendices to Halakhic discussions devoted to subjects that for one reason or another are deemed to intersect with the Halakhah.[3] Second are miscellaneous compositions and composites that stand on their own and do not intersect with the Halakhic program that defines the main beams of the Gemara's construction. We concentrate on those that conduct a dialogue with the Halakhah.

II. How the Halakhah and the Aggadah Cohere in Theology

The theology that surfaces in details in the Talmud[4] and that forms the foundations of the formative documents of Rabbinic Judaism works out the implications of the conviction that the one and only God who created heaven and earth has established a world-order of justice. It wants to explain the way things are in contrast to how they are supposed to be.

The Aggadah recapitulates the story of Adam and Eden in the narrative of Israel and the Land, systematically addressing issues of sin and atonement, Israel and the nations, God and humanity created, as God says, "in our image, after our likeness" (Gen. 1:26). That means, God reveals and humanity comprehends. The Halakhah participates in that same story as it asks how in the construction of the Godly community justice shapes world order as the Torah requires. It spells out the norms for that holy community, which now and in the world to come, Israel is supposed to embody. And both the Halakhah and the Aggadah work out the implications of Scripture's account of the human condition, start to finish. That fact highlights how important is the Talmud's union of the two media of thought and expression. In section vii we shall see how the two media of thought and expression cohere.

The main point is simple. Each mode of discourse undertakes a particular task in the larger exposition of monotheism through myth, that is, truth in narrative form. The Aggadah speaks in large and general terms to the world at large, while the Halakhah uses small and particular rules to speak to the everyday concerns of

2. The Talmud's Theological Framework

ordinary Israelites. The Aggadah recapitulates the story of Israel and its situation among the nations. The Halakhah contemplates Israel in its household, in the Land, in eternity, out of all relationship with the nations but in a timeless realm of unchanging perfection, or aspiring thereto (on the Sabbath, on secular days, respectively, in a condition of purity or aiming thereat). The Aggadah addresses the exteriorities, the Halakhah, the interiorities, of Israel in relationship with God. Categorically, the Aggadah faces outward, toward humanity in general and correlates, shows the relationship of, humanity in general and Israel in particular.

III. THE MONOTHEIST SYSTEM OF RABBINIC JUDAISM: THE MAIN COMPONENTS AND HOW THEY COHERE

Let me attempt to state the theological facts with the simplicity that is appropriate to monotheism.

A religion of numerous gods finds many solutions to one problem, a religion of only one God presents one to many. Life is seldom fair. Rules rarely work. To explain the reason why, polytheisms adduce multiple causes of chaos, a god per anomaly. Diverse gods do various things, so, it stands to reason, ordinarily outcomes conflict.

Monotheism by nature explains many things in a single way. One God rules. Life is meant to be fair, and just rules are supposed to describe what is ordinary, all in the name of that one and only God. So in monotheism a simple logic governs to limit ways of making sense of things. But that logic contains its own dialectics. The tension inherent in the logic of monotheism is simply stated: If one true God has done everything, then, since he is God all-powerful and omniscient, all things are credited to, and blamed on, him. In that case, reality beyond what it is, he can be either good or bad, just or unjust — but not both.

Responding to the dialectics of monotheism, the Aggadah systematically reveals the justice of the one and only God of all creation. God is not only God but also good. Appealing to the facts of Scripture, the Written part of the Torah, in the documents of the Oral part of the Torah, the sages in the first six centuries of the Common Era constructed a coherent theology, a cogent structure and logical system, to expose the justice of God. That identifies the *logos* of God — the logic that renders systematic and coherent the account of God made manifest in the Torah, Written and Oral, as set forth by sages in its originally-oral, memorized component..

The theology of the Aggadah expressed episodically in the Midrash-compilations and in the Talmud's Aggadic components conveys the picture of world order based on God's justice and equity. The categorical structure of the Aggadah encompasses the components, in sequential order: God and man; the Torah; Israel and the nations. The working-system of the Aggadah finds its dynamic in the struggle between God's plan for creation — to create a perfect world of justice — and man's will. That dialectics embodies in a single paradigm the events contained in the sequences, rebellion, sin, punishment, repentance, and atonement; exile and return; or the disruption of world order and the restoration of world order. The Halakhah manifestly means to form Israel in particular into the embodiment of God's plan for a perfect world of justice, and corresponds in its principal divisions to the three categories of the Aggadic theology, of which more presently. Let me set forth a somewhat more elaborate synopsis of the same story in these few, still-simple propositions:

[1] God formed creation in accord with a plan, which the Torah reveals. World order can be shown by the facts of nature and society set forth in that plan to conform to a pattern of reason based upon justice. Those who possess the Torah — Israel — know God and those who do not — the gentiles — reject him in favor of idols. What happens to each of the two sectors of humanity, respectively, responds to their relationship with God. Israel in the present age is subordinate to the nations, because God has designated the gentiles as the medium for penalizing Israel's rebellion, meaning through Israel's subordination and exile to provoke Israel to repent (Chapter Five). Private life as much as the public order conforms to the principle that God rules justly in a creation of perfection and stasis.

[2] The perfection of creation, realized in the rule of exact justice, is signified by the timelessness of the world of human affairs, their conformity to a few enduring paradigms that transcend change (theology of history). No present, past, or future marks time, but only the recapitulation of those patterns. Perfection is further embodied in the unchanging relationships of the social commonwealth (theology of political economy), which assure that scarce resources, once allocated, remain in stasis. A further indication of perfection lies in the complementarity of the components of creation, on the one side, and, finally, the correspondence between God and man, in God's image (theological anthropology), on the other.

[3] Israel's condition, public and personal, marks flaws in creation. What disrupts perfection is the sole power capable of standing on its own against God's power, and that is man's will. What man controls and God cannot coerce is man's capacity to form intention and therefore choose either arrogantly to defy, or humbly to love, God. Because man defies God, the sin that results from man's rebellion flaws creation and disrupts world order (theological theodicy). The paradigm of the rebellion of Adam in Eden governs, the act of arrogant rebellion leading to exile from Eden thus accounting for the condition of humanity. But, as in the original transaction of alienation and consequent exile, God retains the power to encourage repentance through punishing man's arrogance (Chapter Six). In mercy, moreover, God exercises the power to respond to repentance with forgiveness, that is, a change of attitude evoking a counterpart change. Since, commanding his own will, man also has the power to initiate the process of reconciliation with God, through repentance, an act of humility, man may restore the perfection of that order that through arrogance he has marred.

2. The Talmud's Theological Framework

[4] God ultimately will restore that perfection that embodied his plan for creation (Chapter Seven). In the work of restoration death that comes about by reason of sin will die, the dead will be raised and judged for their deeds in this life, and most of them, having been justified, will go on to eternal life in the world to come. In the paradigm of man restored to Eden is realized in Israel's return to the Land of Israel. In that world or age to come, however, that sector of humanity that through the Torah knows God will encompass all of humanity. Idolaters will perish, and humanity that comprises Israel at the end will know the one, true God and spend eternity in his light.

Now, recorded in this way, the story that emerges from the Aggadah — monotheism in mythic form — proves remarkably familiar, with its stress on God's justice (to which his mercy is integral), man's correspondence with God in his possession of the power of will, man's sin of rebellion against God and God's response. If we translate into the narrative of Israel, from the beginning to the calamity of the destruction of the (first) Temple, the picture of matters that is set forth in both abstract and concrete ways in the Aggadah, we turn out to state the human condition in terms of Israel. Then we find a reprise of the Authorized History laid out in Genesis through Kings and amplified by the principal prophets. the Israelite set his will against God's word, sinned, and was exiled from Eden. the Israelite's counterpart, Israel formed by the Torah, entered the Land, sinned, and was exiled from the Land.

The generative categories defined just now prove not only imperative and irreducible but also logically sequential. Each of the four parts of my account of the theology of the Aggadah — [1] the perfectly just character of world order, [2] indications of its perfection, [3] sources of its imperfection, [4] means for the restoration of world order and the result of the restoration — belongs in its place and set in any other sequence the four units become incomprehensible. Further, each component of the whole in order, drawing upon its predecessor, pointing toward its successor, forms part of an unfolding story that can be told in only one direction and in the dictated order and in no other way. Shift the position of a generative component and place it before or after some other, and the entire flow of thought is disrupted. That is the mark of a well-crafted theology, a coherent structure, a compelling system. these focus upon the condition of holy Israel in relationship to God, community, and self.

IV. THE AGGADIC DIMENSION: ISRAEL IN THE WORLD. GENESIS RABBAH XIX:IX.1-2

The theological system of a just world order answerable to one God animates the Aggadah. The single narrative logic that encompasses the entire system is captured in the following composition concerning Adam and Israel, their parallel stories. Adam stands for humanity at large, Israel for that portion of humanity formed by acceptance of the Torah of Sinai. The matter is stated in Genesis Rabbah, a commentary on the book of Genesis, which reached closure in ca. 450 C.E., and in Chapter Five we shall see how the Talmud joins the Halakhic and the Aggadic components of the same doctrine.

Genesis Rabbah XIX:IX.1-2

2. A. R. Abbahu in the name of R. Yosé bar Haninah: "It is written, 'But they [Israel] are like a man [Adam], they have transgressed the covenant' (Hos. 6:7).
   B. "'They are like a man,' specifically, like the first man. [We shall now compare the story of the first man in Eden with the story of Israel in its land.]

Now the sage identifies God's action in regard to Adam with a counterpart action in regard to Israel, in each case matching verse for verse, beginning with Eden and Adam. Adam is brought to Eden as Israel is brought to the Land, with comparable outcomes:

   C. "'In the case of the first man, I brought him into the garden of Eden, I commanded him, he violated my commandment, I judged him to be sent away and driven out, but I mourned for him, saying "How..."' [which begins the book of Lamentations, hence stands for a lament, but which, as we just saw, also is written with the consonants that also yield, 'Where are you'].
   D. "'I brought him into the garden of Eden,' as it is written, 'And the Lord God took the man and put him into the garden of Eden' (Gen. 2:15).
   E. "'I commanded him,' as it is written, 'And the Lord God commanded...' (Gen. 2:16).
   F. "'And he violated my commandment,' as it is written, 'Did you eat from the tree concerning which I commanded you' (Gen. 3:11).
   G. "'I judged him to be sent away,' as it is written, 'And the Lord God sent him from the garden of Eden' (Gen. 3:23).
   H. "'And I judged him to be driven out.' 'And he drove out the man' (Gen. 3:24).
   I. "'But I mourned for him, saying, "How...".' 'And he said to him, "Where are you"' (Gen. 3:9), and the word for 'where are you' is written, 'How....'

Now comes the systematic comparison of Adam and Eden with Israel and the Land of Israel:

   J. "'So too in the case of his descendants, [God continues to speak,] I brought them [Israel] into the Land of Israel, I commanded them, they violated my commandment, I judged them to be sent out and driven away but I mourned for them, saying, "How...."'"

2. The Talmud's Theological Framework 19

K. "'I brought them into the Land of Israel.' 'And I brought you into the land of Carmel' (Jer. 2:7).
L. "'I commanded them.' 'And you, command the children of Israel' (Ex. 27:20). 'Command the children of Israel' (Lev. 24:2).
M. "'They violated my commandment.' 'And all Israel have violated your Torah' (Dan. 9:11).
N. "'I judged them to be sent out.' 'Send them away, out of my sight and let them go forth' (Jer 15:1).
O. "'....and driven away.' 'From my house I shall drive them' (Hos. 9:15).
P. "'But I mourned for them, saying, "How...."' 'How has the city sat solitary, that was full of people' (Lam. 1:1)."

We end with Lamentations, the writing of mourning produced after the destruction of the Temple in Jerusalem in 586 by the Babylonians. Here we end where we began, Israel in exile from the Land, like Adam in exile from Eden. But the Torah is clear that there is a difference, which we shall address in its proper place: Israel can repent.

These persons, Israel and Adam, form not individual and particular, one time characters, but exemplary categories. Israel is Adam's counterpart, Israel is the other model for the Israelite, the one being without the Torah, the other possessing, and possessed by the Torah. Adam's failure defined Israel's task, marked the occasion for the formation of Israel. Israel came into existence in the aftermath of the failure of Creation with the fall of the Adam and his ultimate near-extinction; in the restoration that followed the Flood, God identified Abraham to found in the Land, the new Eden, a supernatural social entity to realize his will in creating the world. Called, variously, a family, a community, a nation, a people, Israel above all embodies God's abode in humanity, his resting place on earth.[5]

The theological system is one that specifically, sets forth the parallel stories of humanity and Israel. Each begins with Eden (the counterpart for Israel being the Land of Israel). The tale of each is marked by sin and punishment (Adam's, Israel's respective acts of rebellion against God, the one through disobedience, the other through violating the Torah). The parallel histories unfold in suffering the penalty of exile for the purpose of bringing about repentance and atonement (Adam from Eden, Israel from the Land). These same stories come together for humanity through Israel, with humanity's restoration to Eden taking place in Israel's return to the Land of Israel and Israel's recovery of eternal life for those who regain Eden/the Land. The dialectics of the tale — the conflict of God's word and man's will — resolve themselves in that narrative, which holds together all of the details of the Aggadic reading of Scripture.

The Rabbinic system therefore takes as its critical problematic the comparison of Israel with the Torah and the nations with idolatry, as we shall see in Chapter Five. It comes to a climax in showing how the comparable stories intersect and diverge at the grave. Israel enjoys the power of repentance (Chapter Six). For from there Israel is destined to the resurrection, judgment, and eternity (the world to come), the nations (that is, the idolaters to the end) to death (Chapter Seven). When we examine the category-formations of the Halakhah, by contrast, what we shall see is an account of Israel not in its external relationship to the nations but viewed wholly on its own. The lines of structure impart order from within. So the Halakhah portrays intransitive Israel, focusing upon its inner life, the Aggadah, transitive Israel, intersecting with the world beyond the sacred. That fact further explains why the category-formation of the Aggadah does not correspond with that of the Halakhah. Each formation is responds to the rules of construction of the same social order — God's justice — but the Aggadic one concerns Israel's social order in the context of God's transaction with humanity, the other, Israel's social order articulated within its own interior architectonics, thus, the one, transitive, the other, intransitive.

The theology of the Aggadah that the Aggadic documents, and Aggadic segments of Halakhic ones (with special reference to the Talmud especially) portray focuses our attention upon one perspective and neglects the other. The outward-facing theology that coheres in the Aggadic documents and compositions of the Talmud investigates the logic of creation, the fall, the regeneration made possible by the Torah, the separation of Israel and the Torah from the nations and idolatry, the one for life through repentance and resurrection, the other for death, and the ultimate restoration of creation's perfection attempted with Adam at Eden, but now through Israel in the Land of Israel. Encompassing the whole of humanity that knows God in the Torah and rejects idolatry, Israel encompasses nearly the whole of humanity, along with nearly the whole of the Israel of the epoch of the Torah and of the Messiah that has preceded. The Aggadah tells about Israel in the context of humanity, and hence speaks of exteriorities. Its perspectives are taken up at the border between outside and inside, the position of standing at the border inside and looking outward: [1] God and the world, [2] the Torah, and [3] Israel and the nations. These form the organizing categories of the Aggadah. They meet their counterparts in the Halakhah.

That other perspective, the one gained by standing at the border, inside and looking still deeper within, responds to the same logic, seeking the coherence and rationality of all things. That perspective focuses upon relationships too. But now they are not those between God and humanity or Israel and the nations, but the ones involving, as already indicated, the following: [1] God and Israel, [2] Israel in its own terms, and [3] the Israelite in his own situation, that is, within the household in particular. If, then, the Aggadah answers the questions posed to justice by Israel's relationships with the world beyond, the Halakhah responds to a different set of questions, also precipitated by the generative problematic of God's justice in an imperfect universe. To complete the theological account, Aggadah having accomplished its task, the logic of a coherent whole requires that the Halakhah

2. The Talmud's Theological Framework

describe interior Israel. That logic must answer the questions posed to justice by Israel's relationships within itself.

When we ask the Aggadic documents and Aggadic passages of Halakhic ones to state their main purpose, it emerges with great force. They set forth a world-view, a way of life, and a theory of the social order, that all together respond to God's presence in the here and now. The purpose of the Torah as the Rabbinic sages expound the Torah is to reveal God's justice, that is to say, the just and rational character of the world order that God has created and now sustains and will ultimately perfect. Let me spell out the religious system of the Aggadah that attains full and systematic exposure in its theology. It begins with the single, all-sustaining dogma of monotheism — God is one, omnipotent, and just — and spins out the inner logic of that dogma in response to the dialectics inherent therein.

v. The Halakhic Dimension: Israel at Home

The Halakhic complement embodies the extension of God's design for world order into the inner-facing relationships. Specifically, the Halakhah must respond to issues posed by the monotheism of justice to [1] Israel's relationships with God when these relationships do not take place in the intersection of God, Israel, and the nations, but within Israel's own frame of reference, which is to say, the Torah and its laws; and [2] to Israelites' relationships with one another; and [3] to the interior life of the individual Israelite household on its own, with God. If, then, we wish to explore the interiority of Israel in relationship with God, as a shared order, and of Israel's autonomous building block, the household, we are required to take up the norms of everyday conduct that define Israel and signify its sanctification. These norms prevail through time differentiated only by the giving of the Torah at Sinai, destruction of the Temple, and the recovery of eternal life and of Eden/the Land at the end of time. They prevail through space differentiated only between the Land of Israel and everywhere else.

Norms of conduct, more than norms of conviction, served to convey the sages' interior statement. The Halakhah, as we saw in Chapters One through Three, presents a systematic, continuous and orderly picture; it entails dense and intense writing; above all, in sages' entire corpus it is the sole arena of dialectics. The Halakhah and its analysis and exposition involve articulated tension and conflict, demanding lavish expenditure of intellectual energy. And from the closure of the Talmud to our own day, those who mastered the documents of the Aggadah themselves insisted upon the priority of the Halakhah, which is clearly signaled as normative, over the Aggadah, which commonly is not treated as normative in the same way as is the Halakhah The sages represent as encompassing and coherent the entirety of the Halakhah itself, detail by detail. That is why in their magnum opus, the Talmud, they insist upon the harmony of the parts, the cogency of the whole. Details exemplify the whole, the system all together speaks the same message through details.

VI. How the Halakhah Realizes the Aggadah: The Case of the Halakhah of the Fruit of a Tree in the First Three Years after it is Planed, Tractate 'Orlah. Sifra CCII.I.1

The Halakhah from its initial category-formation forms a system of action-symbols. That is to say, actions embodied convictions; they effected the physicalization and empowerment of religious thinking. From patterns of behavior, therefore, we see the outlines of paradigms of belief. No detail lacks its place in the context of the coherent system, none lacks a contribution to make to the articulation of that system.

To give a single instance of that fact, let me introduce the case of the Halakhic presentation, in the Mishnah, Tosefta, and legal-exegetical study of the book of Leviticus called Sifra, of the prohibition against eating the fruit of a fruit-tree for the first three years after it is planted, and the imperative that the fruit in the fourth year after planting be brought to Jerusalem and consumed there. The exposition of the law by Sifra carries us far from the pages of the Talmud of Babylonia, which has no exposition of Mishnah-tractate 'Orlah, but captures the Talmud's approach to the Halakhah: its systematic quality and its theological focus.

The theology of the Halakhah as an interior structure takes up the theme of God's ownership of the Holy Land in relationship to Israel's possession of the Land. God as the ultimate owner of the Land sets the terms of Israel's utilization of the Land. Among the rules that he imposes form the condition of Israel's tenure on the land, Scripture states explicitly, produce of orchards in the first three years after they are planted is "not be eaten. In the fourth year all its fruit shall be set aside for jubilation before the Lord, and only in the fifth year may you use its fruit, that its yield to you may be increased: I am the Lord your God" (Lev. 19:23-25). The yield of the Land responds to Israel's obedience to God's rules for cultivating the Land, and that having been said, why this particular rule carries with it the stated consequence hardly matters. God relates to Israel through the Land and the arrangements that he imposes upon the Land. What happens to Israel in the Land takes the measure of that relationship.

But apart from these traits that characterize all Halakhah of enlandisement, the Halakhah of 'Orlah makes points particular to the topic at hand — and accessible, indeed, possible, only within the framework of that topic. The specificities of the law turn out to define with some precision a message on the relationship of Israel to the Land of Israel and to God. And that message intersects with the mythic formulation of monotheism in the story of Adam and Eve and their loss of Eden. What is in play is the theme of the restoration of humanity to Eden through the presence of Israel in the Land of Israel.

If we turn to Sifra Chapter CCII:I.1, our attention is drawn to a number of quite specific traits of the law of 'Orlah, and these make explicit matters of religious conviction that we might otherwise miss. The first is that the prohibition of 'Orlah-

2. The Talmud's Theological Framework

fruit applies solely within the Land of Israel and not to the neighboring territories occupied by Israelites, which means that, once again, it is the union of Israel with the Land of Israel that invokes the prohibition:

Sifra CCII:I.1

A. "When you come [into the land and plant all kinds of trees for food, then you shall count their fruit as forbidden; three years it shall be forbidden to you, it must not be eaten. And in the fourth year all their fruit shall be holy, an offering of praise to the Lord. But in the fifth year you may eat of their fruit, that they may yield more richly for you: I am the Lord your God" (Lev. 19:23-25).]
B. Might one suppose that the law applied once they came to Transjordan?
C. Scripture says, "...into the land,"
D. the particular Land [of Israel].

What that means is that some trait deemed to inhere in the Land of Israel and no other territory must define the law, and a particular message ought to inhere in this law. This same point registers once more: it is only trees that Israelites plant in the Land that are subject to the prohibition, not those that gentiles planted before the Israelites inherited the land:

Sifra CCII:I.2

A. "When you come into the land and plant":
B. excluding those that gentiles have planted prior to the Israelites' coming into the land.
C. Or should I then exclude those that gentiles planted even after the Israelites came into the land?
D. Scripture says, "all kinds of trees."

A further point of special interest requires that the Israelite plant the tree as an act of deliberation; if the tree merely grows up on its own, it is not subject to the prohibition. So Israelite action joined to Israelite intention is required:

Sifra CCII:I.4

A. "...and plant...":
B. excluding one that grows up on its own.
C. "...and plant...":
D. excluding one that grows out of a grafting or sinking a root.

The several points on which Sifra's reading of the Halakhah and the verses of Scripture that declare the Halakhah alert us to a very specific religious principle embedded in the Halakhah of 'Orlah.

First, the law takes effect only from the point at which Israel enters the land. That is to say, the point of Israel's entry into the Land marks the beginning of the Land's consequential fecundity. In simpler language, the fact that trees produce fruit matters only from Israel's entry onward. To see what is at stake, we recall that the entry of Israel into the Land marks the restoration of Eden (and will again, within the restorationist theology), so there is no missing the point. The Land bears fruit of which God takes cognizance only when the counterpart-moment of creation has struck. The Halakhah has no better way of saying, the entry of Israel into the Land compares with the moment at which the creation of Eden took place — and in no other way does the Halakhah make that point. 'Orlah-law marks the time of the creation of produce from the moment of Israel's entry into the land. Israel's entry into the Land marks a new beginning, comparable to the very creation of the world, just as the Land at the end matches Eden at the outset.

Second, Israelite intentionality is required to subject a tree to the 'Orlah-rule. If an Israelite does not plant the tree with the plan of producing fruit, then the tree is not subject to the rule. If the tree grows up on its own, not by the act and precipitating intentionality of the Israelite, the 'Orlah-rule does not apply. If an Israelite does not plant the tree to produce fruit, the 'Orlah-rule does not apply. And given the character of creation, which marks the norm, the tree must be planted in the ordinary way; if grafted or sunk as a root, the law does not apply. In a moment, this heavy emphasis upon Israelite intentionality will produce a critical result. But first let us ask some more fundamental questions.

What is the counterpart to Israelite observance of the restraint of three years? And why should Israelite intentionality play so critical a role, since, Sifra itself notes, the 'Orlah-rule applies to trees planted even by gentiles? The answer becomes obvious when we ask another question: Can we think of any other commandments concerning fruit-trees in the Land that — sages say time and again — is Eden? Of course we can: "Of every tree of the garden you are free to eat; but as for the tree of knowledge of good and evil, you must not eat of it" (Gen. 2:16). But the Halakhah of 'Orlah imposes upon Israel a more demanding commandment. Of *no* tree in the new Eden may Israel eat for three years after planting. That demands considerable restraint.

Not only so, but it is Israel's own intentionality — not God's — that imposes upon every fruit-bearing tree — and not only the one of Eden — the prohibition of three years. So once Israel wants the fruit, it must show that it can restrain its desire and wait for three years. By Israel's act of will, Israel has imposed upon itself the requirement of restraint. Taking the entry-point as our guide, we may say that, from the entry into the Land and for the next three years, trees that Israelites value for their fruit and plant with the produce in mind must be left untouched. And, for all time thereafter, when Israelites plant fruit-trees, they must recapitulate that same exercise of self-restraint, that is, act as though, for the case at hand, they have just come into the Land.

To find the context in which these rules make their statement, we consider details, then the main point. First, why three years in particular? Fruit trees were created on the third day of creation. Then, when Israel by intention and action designates a tree — any tree — as fruit-bearing, Israel must wait for three years, as creation waited for three years.

Then the planting of every tree imposes upon Israel the occasion to meet once more the temptation that the first Adam could not overcome. Israel now recapitulates the temptation of Adam then, but Israel, the New Adam, possesses, and is possessed by, the Torah. By its own action and intention in planting fruit trees, Israel finds itself in a veritable orchard of trees like the tree of knowledge of good and evil. The difference between Adam and Israel — permitted to eat all fruit but one, Adam ate the forbidden fruit, while Israel refrains for a specified span of time from fruit from all trees — marks what has taken place, which is the regeneration of humanity. The enlandisement of the Halakhah bears that very special message, and how better make that statement through law than in the explicit concern sages register for the fruit-trees of the Land of Israel. No wonder, then, that 'Orlah-law finds its position, in the Priestly Code, in the rules of sanctification.

So when Israel enters the Land, in exactly the right detail Israel recapitulates the drama of Adam in Eden, but with this formidable difference. The outcome is not the same. By its own act of will Israel addresses the temptation of Adam and overcomes the same temptation, not once but every day through time beyond measure. Adam could not wait out the week, but Israel waits for three years — as long as God waited in creating fruit trees. Adam picked and ate. But here too there is a detail not to be missed. even after three years, Israel may not eat the fruit wherever it chooses. Rather, in the fourth year from planting, Israel will still show restraint, bringing the fruit only "for jubilation before the Lord" in Jerusalem. That signals that the once-forbidden fruit is now eaten in public, not in secret, before the Lord, as a moment of celebration. That detail too recalls the Fall and makes its comment upon the horror of the fall. That is, when Adam ate the fruit, he shamefully hid from God for having eaten the fruit. But when Israel eats the fruit, it does so proudly, joyfully, before the Lord. The contrast is not to be missed, so too the message. Faithful Israel refrains when it is supposed to, and so it has every reason to cease to refrain and to eat "before the Lord." It has nothing to hide, and everything to show.

And there is more. In the fifth year Israel may eat on its own, the time of any restraint from enjoying the gifts of the Land having ended. That sequence provides fruit for the second Sabbath of creation, and so through time. How so? Placing Adam's sin on the first day after the first Sabbath, thus Sunday, then calculating the three forbidden years as Monday, Tuesday, and Wednesday of the second week of creation, reckoning on the jubilation of Thursday, we come to the Friday, eve of the second Sabbath of creation. So now, a year representing a day of the Sabbatical week, just as Leviticus says so many times in connection with the Sabbatical year, the three prohibited years allow Israel to show its true character, fully regenerate, wholly and humbly accepting God's commandment, the one Adam broke. And the rest follows.

Here, then, is the message of the 'Orlah-Halakhah, the statement that only through the details of the laws of 'Orlah as laid out in both parts of the Torah, written and oral, the Halakhah could hope to make. By its own act of restraint, the New Adam, Israel, in detailed action displays its repentance in respect to the very sin that the Old Adam committed, the sin of disobedience and rebellion. Facing the same opportunity to sin, Israel again and again over time refrains from the very sin that cost Adam Eden. So by its manner of cultivation of the Land and its orchards, Israel manifests what in the very condition of humanity has changed by the giving of the Torah: the advent of humanity's second chance, through Israel. Only in the Land that succeeds Eden can Israel, succeeding Adam, carry out the acts of regeneration that the Torah makes possible.

The Halakhah thus sets forth a statement of the same religious structure and system that the Aggadah is asked to portray. The unity of the two media of religious thought and expression comes about by reason of their complementarity: each accomplishes one half of the whole task that sages take for themselves. The Halakhah, normative law, makes the same statement in terms of behavior that Aggadah in its systematic and abstract mode makes in terms of beliefs. Each statement, the Aggadic one, the Halakhic one, addressed a distinct realm of Israel's existence, the one exteriorities, the other interiorities. Specifically, the Aggadah addresses issues of transcendence, the Halakhah, those of immanence. That is expressed in so many words in the Halakhic corpus itself, when a sage declares that what God possesses in this world, with the Temple in ruins, is only the four cubits of the Halakhah — that alone. In that context, we see what is at stake in the theological expositions of the law as shown in Chapters Six, Seven, and Eight.

VII. THE HALAKHIC REALIZATION OF THE AGGADIC THEOLOGY SEEN WHOLE: ACTUALIZING THE TORAH'S STORY

The theological narrative of the Halakhah viewed whole as a system may be briefly summarized as a whole in a few sentences, in two paragraphs, the one describing the problem facing God in the encounter with the Israelite, the other the solution put forth at Sinai through the Halakhic account of the regenerate social order Israel is to realize.

1. THE THEOLOGICAL PROBLEM: God created nature as the setting for his encounter with humanity. Creation was meant as God's Kingdom for the Israelite's bliss. But with the sin of the Israelite committed in rebellion against God's will, the loss of Eden, and the advent of death began the long quest for the regeneration of the Israelite. In the unfolding of generations, ten from Adam to Noah, ten from Noah to Abraham and thence to Sinai, it was only Israel that presented itself for the encounter. But then Israel too showed itself no different from Adam. For on the other side of Sinai came the celebration of the Golden Calf.

2. The Talmud's Theological Framework

2. THE HALAKHIC SOLUTION: What to do now? It is to rebuild God's Kingdom among that sector of humanity that undertakes to respond to God's self-manifestation in the torah and to realize God's dominion and imperatives: the Torah, the commandments. God provided for Israel, surrogate of humanity, the commandments as a medium of sanctification for the reconciliation with God and renewal of Eden, the triumph over the grave. Freed of sin through offerings that signified obedience to God's will, by reason of repentance and atonement, signifying man's acceptance of God's will over his own, which to begin with had brought about the fall from Eden, man might meet God, the two in mutual and reciprocal commitment. Where Israel atoned for sin and presented itself as ready for the meeting, there God and Israel would found their Eden, not a place but an occasion. In overcoming the forces of death and affirming life through purity, Israel brings into being such an occasion. The Halakhah then serves as the medium of sanctification of Israel in the here-and-now, in preparation for the salvation of Israel and its restoration to Eden.

The Halakhah lays out how Israel's entire social order may be constructed to realize the situation represented by Eden now and to restore Eden then. But it would be this time through the willing realization of God's rule, both in the present hour and at the end of days. That actualization takes place within Israel. How will it happen? Tutored by the Torah to want by nature what God wants but will not coerce them to want — "the commandments were given only to purify the heart of man" — Israel makes itself able to realize God's will and to form his kingdom within its holy community. Through examining the Halakhah in its native categories or tractates, these propositions are shown to animate the entire Halakhic corpus, which is thus proved to embody a theological system, one that rests firmly upon the foundations of Scripture whole and in detail.

In fact, we have in the Halakhah a reworking of two parallel stories, the story of the creation and fall of Adam and Eve from Eden, then the story of the regeneration of humanity through the Torah's formation of Israel. The two stories then are linked in the encounter of Israel and the nations, represented by the uncleanness of death that, through the disciplines of purity, Israel is to over come. The tension between them comes to its resolution in the resurrection of Israel, from death, those who know God being destined for eternal life. The two stories, adumbrated in the lower-case-caps bearing Roman numerals that form the heads of the outline that follows, represent the native category-formations of the Aggadah, and, as is clear, the native category-formations of the Halakhah, in ordinary type bearing Arabic numerals, as its categories expounded in the following outline are folded into the Aggadic framework:

I. THE STORY OF MAN AND REBELLION, SIN AND ATONEMENT, EXILE AND RESTORATION
    1. Where and When Is Eden?
    2. Who Owns Eden?

II. THE PARALLEL STORY: ISRAEL AND GOD, SIN AND JUST PUNISHMENT, REPENTANCE AND ATONEMENT, FORGIVENESS AND RESTORATION
  3. Israel's Adam and Eve
  4. Sin and Atonement
  5. Intentionality and the Civil Order
III. THE STORY OF ISRAEL AND THE NATIONS, SPECIFICALLY, ISRAEL AND THE TORAH, THE GENTILES LACKING THE TORAH
  6. Enemies of Eden, Tangible and Invisible
  7. The Contest between Death and Life
  8. Overcoming Death
  9. The Kingdom of God

The sages' philosophical reading of Scripture — its Halakhah and its Aggadah alike — leads to the transformation of the Torah's account of humanity's story into the design for Israel's social order: God's kingdom, Eden realized now, restored at the end. Now let us recapitulate the main findings derived from the specific category-formations/tractates that we meet in the Mishnah, once more noting that the Talmud covers only some of them.

1. WHERE AND WHEN IS EDEN?
   i. Shebi'it, the Sabbatical year, the Sabbath for the Land
   ii. 'Orlah, the prohibition of the fruit of a tree in the first three years after it is planted
   iii. Kilayim, the prohibition of mixed seeds in the vineyard
   iv. Shabbat-'Erubin, the recapitulation of Eden on the Sabbath day, the sanctification of the day through repose

By Eden Scripture means, that place whole and at rest that God sanctified; "Eden" stands for creation in perfect repose. In the Halakhah Eden stands for not a particular place but nature in a defined condition, at a particular moment: creation in Sabbath repose, sanctified. Then a place in repose at the climax of creation, at sunset at the start of the seventh day, whole and at rest, embodies, realizes Eden. The Halakhah means to systematize the condition of Eden, to define Eden in its normative traits, and also to localize Eden within Israel, the people. How so? Eden is the place to the perfection of which God responded in the act of sanctification at the advent of the seventh day. While the Land in the Written Torah's explicit account of matters, claims the right to repose on the seventh day and in the seventh year of the septennial cycle, it is the location of Israel wherever that may be at the advent of sunset on the eve of the seventh day of the week of creation that recapitulates Eden.

2. WHO OWNS EDEN?
   i. Ma'aserot, tithing
   ii. Terumot, priestly rations

2. The Talmud's Theological Framework

    iii. Hallah, dough offering
    iv. Ma'aser Sheni, second tithe
    v. Bikkurim, first fruits
    vi. Pe'ah, leaving the corner of the field for the poor
    vii. Dema'i, doubtfully-tithed produce

The story expands to within the motif of Eden, the matter of ownership and possession as media for the expression of the relationship between the Israelite and God. God accorded to Adam and Eve possession of nearly everything in Eden, retaining ownership — the right to govern according to his will — for himself. The key to the entire system of interaction between God and Israel through the Land and its gifts emerges in the Halakhah of Ma'aserot and its companions, which deal — along the lines of Shebi'it and 'Erubin — with the difference between possession and ownership. God owns the world, which he made. But God has accorded to man the right of possession of the earth and its produce. This he did twice, once to the Israelite — Adam and Eve — in Eden, the second time to Israel in the Land of Israel. And to learn the lesson that the Israelite did not master, that possession is not ownership but custody and stewardship, Israel has to acknowledge the claims of the creator to the glory of all creation, which is the Land. This Israel does by giving back God's share of the produce of the Land at the time, and in the manner, that God defines. The enlandised components of the Halakhah therefore form a single, cogent statement of matters.

3. ADAM AND EVE
    i. Qiddushin, betrothals
    ii. Ketubot, marriage contracts
    iii. Nedarim, vows
    iv. Nazir, the special vow of the Nazirite
    v. Sotah, the ordeal imposed on the wife suspected of adultery
    vi. Gittin, writs of divorce
    vii. Yebamot, levirate marriages

The Halakhah of the family, covering the act of sanctification of a woman by a man (Qiddushin), the marriage-agreement (Ketubah), vows and special vows, the disposition of a charge of unfaithfulness against a woman, and the severance of the marital bond of sanctification through a writ of divorce or death, does not ubiquitously invoke the metaphor of Adam and Eve in Eden. Our task, then, is to identify the principal foci of that Halakhah and to investigate the appropriate context in which it is to be interpreted. How here does Eden figure? The connection is made articulate by the (possibly later) liturgical framework in which the Halakhah plays itself out. There, in the liturgy of the marriage-canopy, the act of creation of the Israelite is recapitulated, the bride and groom explicitly compared to Adam and Eve. Not only so, but the theme of the Land and Israel intervenes as well — two motifs dominant in the Halakhic theology examined to this point.

4. SIN AND ATONEMENT
   i. Sheqalim, the half-sheqel offering to support the public sacrifices
   ii. Tamid & Yoma, the daily whole offering, the rite of the Day of Atonement
   iii. Zebahim & Menahot, offerings of meat and cereal
   iv. Arakhin, the pledge of valuation
   v. Bekhorot, firstlings
   vi. Meilah, sacrilege
   vii. Temurah, substituting a beast for an already-consecrated beast

The Halakhah takes account of the tragedy of Eden and provides for a new moral entity, a reformed transaction accorded that entity, one not available to Adam and Eve. For God at Eden made no provision for atonement for sin, but, in the unfolding of the Israelite's story, God grasped the full measure of the Israelite's character and drew the necessary conclusion and acted on it. Endowed with autonomous will, the Israelite has the power to rebel against God's will. Therefore the Halakhah finds urgent the question, how is the Israelite, subject to God's rule, to atone for the sin that, by his rebellious nature, the Israelite is likely to commit? The Torah to answer that question formulates the rules that govern the Israelite both [1] when under God's dominion and [2] when in rebellion against God's will. These represent the two aspects of the one story that commences with Eden, leads to the formation of Israel through Abraham, Isaac, and Jacob, God's antidotes to Adam, and climaxes at Sinai. But Israel also is the Israelite, so that story accommodates both Adam's fall and Israel's worship of the golden calf, and, as the denouement, Adam and Eve's exile from Eden and Israel's ultimate exile from the Land. How, then does God propose to repair the world he has made to take account of the Israelite's character and Israel's own proclivity?

5. INTENTIONALITY AND THE CIVIL ORDER
   i. Keritot, sins penalized by extirpation (dying young)
   ii. Sanhedrin-Makkot, the court-system & criminal justice
   iii. Baba Qamma-Baba Mesi'a-Baba Batra, the civil law
   iv. Horayot, when the authorities err in the law
   v. Shebuot, oaths

The Halakhah dictates the character of (its) Israel's civil order — its political institutions and system of criminal justice. It undertakes a labor of differentiation of power, indicating what agency or person has the power to precipitate the working of politics as legitimate violence. When we understand the differentiating force that imparts to politics its activity and dynamism, we grasp the theology that animates the structures of the politics and propels the system. The details of the Halakhah, in particular the sanctions assigned to various infractions,

2. The Talmud's Theological Framework

effect the taxonomy of power, which forms an implicit exegesis of the story of Eden, translated into reflection on the power of intentionality.

6. ENEMIES OF EDEN, TANGIBLE AND INVISIBLE
   i. Tangible Enemies: Abodah Zarah, idolatry
   ii. Invisible Enemies: Death. Ohalot, corpse-uncleanness
   iii. Negaim, the skin-ailment, equivalent to death
   iv. Zabim and Niddah, the uncleanness of flux

The enemies of Eden take shape around the grand struggle between life and death, in the here and now meaning Israel and the gentiles, at the end of days meaning those who will stand in judgment and go onward to the world to come and eternal life, and those who will perish in the grave. Specifically, the world beyond the limits of Israel forms an undifferentiated realm of idolatry and uncleanness. Then how is Israel to negotiate life with the world of gentiles and their idolatry, corpses and their contamination? Among the sources of uncleanness, tangible and invisible, we begin with the gentiles and proceed to corpse- and comparable kinds of uncleanness. But the two — gentiles, corpses — form a single domain. The former bears exactly the same uncleanness as the latter. Gentiles, defined as idolaters, and Israelites, defined as worshippers of the one and only God, part company at death. For the moment Israelites die — only to rise from the grave. Gentiles die for eternity. The roads intersect at the grave, each component of humanity taking its own path beyond. Israelites — meaning, those possessed of right conviction — will rise from the grave, stand in judgment, but then enter upon eternal life, to which no one else will enjoy access.

7. THE CONTEST BETWEEN DEATH AND LIFE
   i. Makhshirin, liquids that render formerly-dry produce susceptible to uncleanness
   ii. Tohorot, cases of doubt in matters of uncleanness
   iii. Uqsin, the uncleanness of parts of produce
   iv. Kelim, uncleanness affecting utensils

The sources of change and disruption that threaten the cleanness, hence the sanctification of the Temple are the same sources that threaten the norm of cleanness of the household. If the same uncleanness affects the Temple and the table, then the only difference is one of degree, not of kind, as the Halakhah states explicitly. And the rest follows. The web of relationships between sanctification and uncleanness spins itself out into every corner of the Israelite household, where the system makes a difference. And it is the will of the householder that determines the difference that the distinction between clean and unclean is going to make. Everything is relative to the householder's will; he has it in his power to draw the household table into alignment with the altar in the Temple, that is to say, to place the table and the food set thereon into relationship, onto a continuum, with the altar and the Holy Things of the cult. This he can accomplish through an act of will that motivates an attitude of constant watchfulness in the household for those very sources of contamination that Scripture identifies as danger to the Lord's altar in the Jerusalem Temple.

8. OVERCOMING DEATH
    i. Parah, preparing purification-water
    ii. Miqvaot, immersion pools
    iii. Tebul Yom, the uncleanness of one who has immersed, which lasts until sunset completes the rite of purification
    iv. Yadayim, the special case of the uncleanness of hands
    v. Hagigah, Home and Temple in Hierarchical Formation

From death and its affect upon food and drink, that is, the uncleanness caused by, and analogous to, death, we turn to the media for the restoration of life. Still water unaffected by human agency restores the natural condition disrupted by uncleanness other than that of the corpse and its analogues, while by contrast purification-water systematically subjected to human intervention — constant attention, deliberate action, start to finish — alone removes corpse-uncleanness. We have then to account for the exclusion of man from the one process, the radical insistence upon his inclusion, in full deliberation, within the other. Uncleanness that comes about by reason of any cause but death and its analogues is removed by the Heaven's own dispensation, not by man's intervention: rain-fall, sunset suffice. Ordinary purification is done by nature, resulting from natural processes. But as to persons and objects that have contracted uncleanness from death, nature on its own cannot produce the kind of water that bears the power to remove that uncleanness and restore the condition of nature. Only man can. And man can do this only by the highest level of concentration, the most deliberate and focussed action. the Israelite's act of will overcomes the uncleanness of death, just as man's act of deliberate rebellion brought about death to begin with. the Israelite restores what man has disrupted. Had the Halakhah wished in its terms and categories to accomplish a reprise of the story of Adam's fall, it could not have made a more eloquent statement than it does in the contrast between the Halakhah of Miqvaot and that of Parah.

9. THE KINGDOM OF GOD
    i. Berakhot, reciting the Shema, the Prayer, and Blessings over food
    ii. Hullin, slaughter of animals for domestic use
    iii. Megillah, the celebration of Purim
    iv. Rosh Hashanah, the celebration of the New Year
    v. Pesahim, the celebration of Passover
    vi. Sukkah, the celebration of Tabernacles
    vii. Mo'ed Qatan, the intermediate days of a week-long festival

2. The Talmud's Theological Framework

  viii. Besah, cooking on festival days
  ix. Ta'anit, special fast days

  As much as the Israelite by his nature rebels against God, the Israelite tutored by the commandments willingly accepts God's will and therefore his rule. What are the Halakhah's media for the reformation, regeneration and renewal, of the Israelite? The Halakhah here legislates for not Eden but the kingdom of God. For Sinai's answer to Eden's question transcends the matter of sin and atonement and encompasses the conduct of the ordinary, everyday life lived under God's rule. The normative deals with the normal, so the final solution to God's dilemma with the Israelite — how to accord the Israelite free will but to nurture in the Israelite freely-given love for God — lies in the Torah. That way of life in accord with God's rule means to form the *Paideia,* the character-building education to transform the Israelite by making Israelite the Israelite's freely-given obedience to God as natural as was the First the Israelite's contumacious rebellion against God. That is why the Halakhic provision for life in God's kingdom moves from the ordinary day and its duties to the table and its everyday nourishment, then to the meeting with God that is seasonal and temporal, and finally to the climax of the system, confrontation with routine crisis.

  Thus brief precis shows how a few large motifs form of the details of the Halakhah a single coherent system, one that tells a story. Clearly, the Halakhah works from Scripture forward. But, being theologians, systematic thinkers, speaking through symbol and myth but intent on a philosophical reading of religion in quest of a coherent, proportionate, and rigorously argued statement, they do not randomly rework this detail or that. Rather, the sages' philosophical reading of Scripture that comes to its climax in the Talmud — its Halakhah and its Aggadah alike — produces a coherent theology. It leads to the transformation of the Torah's account of humanity's story into the detailed design for Israel's social order. The details all find their place within the structure of the whole, and in its workings, the system that sages have constructed animates the whole, the parts working well together to make a simple statement. That is easily set forth. In its actualities Israel embodies — or is meant to embody — God's plan for humanity, not individual, but as a social entity: God's kingdom, Eden both realized in the here and now and restored at the end.

  The Halakhah brings about the transformation of the here and the now, of the particular occasion into the embodiment, the exemplification, of the abstract ground of being. Involved is relationship of realms of the sacred: the rules of engagement between and among God, Land, Israel, time, place, circumstance. Through the fabric of everyday life of the Land lived out in the household, village, and the holy metropolis, Jerusalem (the three dimensions of the social order of which the Halakhah takes account), Eden is read as not historical moment but situation and occasion. That then precipitates thought about the human condition.

But Eden does not impose narrow limits on the amplification of that thought. It is not the only condition.

There is also the situation brought about by the second great theme, besides Eden, that is implicit in the Halakhah. It is God's self-manifestation in the Torah: the occasion for the reform and renewal of humanity through Israel, the counterpart and opposite of the Israelite. The Halakhah therefore begins with Eden but progresses to the realization of God's kingdom within holy Israel's social order, conceiving of Israel both enlandised (defined within the Land) and utopian (located anywhere), as the category of the Halakhah requires.

A third massive motif involves Eden once more, this time under God's rule, and it too engages with the Torah's account of Israel at Sinai. It concerns the re-embodiment of Israel, the restoration that comes about not alone in the end of days when the Messiah comes, but in the here-and-now of the workaday world. It is there that the Israelite formed by the discipline of the Torah learns both to atone for, and to overcome, his natural propensity willfully to rebel against God. Within the social order of an enlandised Israel moral persons construct a godly society. That reading of the Written Torah and translation of its law into the canons of ordinary life speaks in the acutely-present tense to portray for the Israelite a worthy future well within the Israelite's own capacities to realize: "the commandments were given only to purify the heart of the Israelite ," and "All-Merciful wants the heart," as the Talmud frames matters.

Therein I identify the theology of the Halakhah: massive, closed system that, in dialogue with the Aggadah but in its own category-formations and language, says the same thing about many things, numerous details bearing a single message. That message is the actualization in deed of the story of Creation, sin and loss, and of the regeneration of humanity through the Torah and the ultimate restoration of humanity to Eden. Now, in the theological context defined in this chapter, we turn to three cases in which the Talmud's Halakhic and Aggadic compositions work together to make a single statement: theology through law, law through theology, in three cases of fundamental importance.

To conclude: the Talmud forms the apex of the Rabbinic canon of antiquity, therefore, because it alone succeeds in joining Aggadic to Halakhic discourse in the formation of a single coherent, systematic statement. The Halakhah and the Aggadah in specific contexts work out the logic of a single generative conviction. In Chapters Five (theory of the gentiles, theology of history), Six (theory of atonement, theology of humanity's regeneration), and Seven (theory of criminal justice, theology of judgment and restoration at the end of days), we shall examine three primary instances of those contexts and see how the Aggadah's theological principles define the context in which the Halakhic statement is realized.

ENDNOTES

[1] My presentation of the theology that animates the Aggadah is in *The Theology of the Oral Torah. Revealing the Justice of God.* Kingston and Montreal, 1999: McGill-Queen's University Press and Ithaca, 1999: Cornell University Press. The counterpart for the Halakhah is *The Theology of the Halakhah.* Leiden, 2001: E. J. Brill. BRILL REFERENCE LIBRARY OF ANCIENT JUDAISM.

[2] This is a rough estimate, based on a sample of a handful of the thirty-seven tractates. See my *Judaism: The Classical Statement. The Evidence of the Talmud of Babylonia.* Chicago, 1986: University of Chicago Press.

[3] I have identified these in the monograph, *The Talmud of Babylonia's Massive Miscellanies. The Problem of Agglutinative Discourse in the Talmud of Babylonia.* Atlanta, 1992: Scholars Press for South Florida Studies in the History of Judaism, and I have further shown how the juxtaposition of Halakhic and Aggadic expositions accomplishes the compilers' larger propositional goals in *Rationality and Structure: The Talmud of Babylonia's Anomalous Juxtapositions.* Atlanta, 1997: Scholars Press for South Florida Studies in the History of Judaism.

[4] The Aggadah in general, encompassing the Talmud's Aggadic compositions as well as those of the Midrash-compilations of Scriptural exegesis, participates in a larger system of theology and attests to details of that system. To encounter principal statements of the Rabbinic theological system we have to move beyond the limits of the Talmid and consider compositions found in Midrash-compilations. The theological expositions that appear in Midrash-compilations cited below are integral in the system realized, also, in the Talmud.

[5] I hardly need repeat that this definition of "Israel" cannot be confused with any secular meanings attributed to the same word, e.g., nation or ethnic entity, counterpart to other nations or ethnic groups.

3

The Talmud's Union of Halakhah and Aggadah

The Halakhah of Gentile Idolatry and the Aggadah of Gentile Rejection of the Torah

I. ISRAEL AND THE NATIONS

Three parties intersect in the fundamental issue, how is Israel to deal with the gentiles: Scripture, which prohibits interaction with idolatry and those that practice it, the Halakhah of the Mishnah and the Talmud tractate Abodah Zarah, on idolatry, which articulates that principle through concrete rules, and the Aggadah of the same tractate of the Talmud, which systematically sets forth the theology of Israel and the gentiles. The opening pages of tractate Abodah Zarah unite the Halakhah and the Aggadah into a coherent statement. It is simple: Gentiles worship idols, Israelites know the one and only God, and that fact governs all relationships.

Scripture is clear that Israel is to enter into no relationships whatsoever with idolaters. The Halakhah set forth in the Mishnah and articulated in the Talmud defines the gentile world as an undifferentiated realm of idolatry and takes as its task the negotiation between Israelites and the pagan world in which the Israelites, even in the Land of Israel, now live: how are they to conduct themselves in accord with the Torah so that at no point and in no way do they give support to idolatry. In its basic exposition of the theme of idolatry, the Halakhah rests squarely on the foundations of Scripture, supplying rules and regulations that carry out the fundamental Scriptural commandments about destroying idols and everything that has to do with idolatry.

But the Halakhah joined to the Aggadah that we shall survey so formulates matters as to transform the entire topic of idolatry into an essay on Israel's and God's relationships with the gentiles, who are idolaters by definition. The task of

37

the Aggadah as introduced by the Talmud is to explain the foundations of the Halakhah: why are the gentiles rejected by God and therefore abhorred by Israel?

For the Written Torah the community at large forms the focus of the law, and idolatry is not to be negotiated with by the collectivity of holy Israel. In its Land Israel is to wipe out idolatry, even as a memory. Scripture is clear that Israel is to obliterate all mention of idols (Ex. 23:13), not bow down to gentiles' gods or serve them but overthrow them and break them into pieces (Ex. 23:24): "You shall break down their altars and dash in pieces their pillars and hew down their Asherim and burn their graven images with fire" (Deut. 7:5). Israelites are commanded along these same lines:

> "The graven images of their gods you shall burn with fire; you shall not covet the silver or the gold that is on them or take it for yourselves, lest you be ensnared by it; for it is an abomination to the Lord your God. And you shall not bring an abominable thing into your house and become accused like it"
>
> Deut. 7:25-26
>
> "You shall surely destroy all the places where the nations whom you shall dispossess served their gods, upon the high mountains and upon the hills and under every green tree; you shall tear down their altars and dash in pieces their pillars and burn their Asherim with fire; you shall hew down the graven images of their gods and destroy their name out of that place" (
>
> Deut. 12:2-3

Accordingly, so far as the Written Torah supplies the foundations for the treatment of the matter by the Talmud, the focus of discourse concerning the gentiles is idolatry. Scripture's law does not contemplate Israel's co-existing, in the Land, with gentiles and their idolatry. But the Halakhah speaks to a world that is not so simple. The Land belongs to Israel, but gentiles live there too — and run things. And Israel no longer forms a coherent collectivity but a realm made up of individuals, with their distinctive and particular interests. The Halakhah set forth by the Mishnah and amplified by the Talmud commences its treatment of the same subject with the opposite premise: gentiles live side by side (whether or not in the Land of Israel) with Israelites, and Israelites have to sort out the complex problems of co-existence with idolatry. And that co-existence involves not whole communities, the People, Israel, and the peoples, whoever they may be, but individuals, this Israelite living side by side with that gentile.

Not only so, but the Talmud uses the occasion of idolatry to contemplate a condition entirely beyond the imagination of Scripture, which is the hegemony of idolatrous nations and the subjugation of holy Israel. The Talmud, fully considered, makes of the discussion of idolatry the occasion for the discussion of Israel's place among the nations of the world and of Israel's relationships with gentiles. Furthermore, the Talmud's theory of who Israel is finds its context in the contrast

3. The Talmud's Union of Halakhah and Aggadah...

with the gentiles. The meeting point with the Written Torah is defined by the indicative trait of the gentiles, which is their idolatry; that is all that matters about them. But, as we shall now see, while the Halakhah expounds the local details of everyday relationships with gentiles, the Aggadah of the same Talmud vastly expands the range of thought and takes up the more profound issues of theology of history: gentile dominance in this age, Israel's subjugated position, the power of the idolaters, and the like. So the Aggadah deals with the world at large, the Halakhah, the world at home.

Specifically, the Halakhah systematically amplified by the Talmud, deals first with commercial relationships, second, matters pertaining to idols, and finally to the particular prohibition of wine part of which has served as a libation to an idol. The whole is regularized and ordered. There are relationships with gentiles that are absolutely prohibited, particularly occasions of idol-worship; the Halakhah recognizes that these are major commercial events. When it comes to commerce with idolaters Israelites may not sell or in any way benefit from certain things, may sell but may not utilize certain others, and may sell and utilize yet others. Here, we see immediately, the complex and systematic mode of thought that governs the Talmud's treatment of the topic vastly transcends the rather simple conception that animates Scripture's discussion of the same matter. There are these unstated premises within the Halakhah: [1] what a gentile is not likely to use for the worship of an idol is not prohibited; [2] what may serve not as part of an idol but as an appurtenance thereto is prohibited for Israelite use but permitted for Israelite commerce; [3] what serves idolatry is prohibited for use and for benefit. In reflecting upon relationships with the gentiles, meaning, idolaters, the Talmud moreover takes for granted a number of facts. These turn out to yield a single generalization: gentiles are assumed routinely to practice bestiality, murder, and fornication. Further negative stereotypes concerning idolaters occur. The picture of the Halakhah finds its context in the larger theory of idolatry and its ephemeral hegemony that the Aggadah sets forth.

II. BAVLI ABODAH ZARAH 1:1 I.1-33/2A-5B

The relationship between the two components of the Torah may be simply stated: the Written Torah provides instruction on destroying idolatry, in the premise that Israel has the opportunity to do so. The Halakhah explains how to co-exist with idolatry, recognizing that Israel has no choice but to do so. The Aggadah explains why Israel is chosen, the gentiles rejected. The Torah accounts for the one, idolatry for the other, fact. The Talmud commences with a law and I.1 deals with the wording of the Mishnah-rule. Then the fundamental issue is raised: why has God rejected the gentiles.

Bavli Abodah Zarah 1:1 I.1-33/2A-5B

- A. [2A] Before the festivals of gentiles for three days it is forbidden to do business with them.
- B. (1) To lend anything to them or to borrow anything from them.
- C. (2) To lend money to them or to borrow money from them.
- D. (3) To repay them or to be repaid by them.
- E. R. Judah says, "They accept repayment from them, because it is distressing to him."
- F. They said to him, "Even though it is distressing to him now, he will be happy about it later."

I.1
- A. Rab and Samuel [in dealing with the reading of the key word of the Mishnah, translated festival, the letters of which are 'aleph daled, rather than 'ayin daled, which means, calamity]:
- B. *one repeated the formulation of the Mishnah as, "their festivals."*
- C. *And the other repeated the formulation of the Mishnah as "their calamities."*
- D. *The one who repeated the formulation of the Mishnah as "their festivals" made no mistake, and the one who repeated the formulation of the Mishnah as "their calamities" made no mistake.*
- E. *For it is written,* "For the day of their calamity is at hand" (Deut. 32:15).
- F. *The one who repeated the formulation of the Mishnah as "their festivals" made no mistake, for it is written,* "Let them bring their testimonies that they may be justified" (Isa. 43:9).
- G. *And as to the position of him who repeats the formulation of the Mishnah as "their festivals," on what account does he not repeat the formulation of the Mishnah to yield, "their calamities"?*
- H. *He will say to you, "'Calamity' is preferable [as the word choice when speaking of idolatry]."*
- I. *And as to the position of him who repeats the formulation of the Mishnah as "their calamities," on what account does he not repeat the formulation of the Mishnah to yield "their festivals"?*
- J. *He will say to you, "What causes the calamity that befalls them if not their testimony, so testimony is preferable!"*
- K. *And as to the verse,* "Let them bring their testimonies that they may be justified" (Isa. 43:9), *is this written with reference to gentiles? Lo, it is written in regard to Israel.*
    - L. For said R. Joshua b. Levi, "All of the religious duties that Israelites carry out in this world come and give testimony in their behalf in the world to come: 'Let them bring their witnesses that they may be justified' (Isa. 43:9), that is, Israel; 'and let them hear and say, It is truth' (Isa. 43:9) — this refers to gentiles."
- M. *Rather, said R. Huna b. R. Joshua, "He who formulates the Mishnah to refer to their calamities derives the reading from this verse:* 'They that fashion a graven image are all of them vanity, and their delectable things shall not profit, and their own witnesses see not nor know' (Isa. 44:9)."

3. The Talmud's Union of Halakhah and Aggadah...

The Halakhic exposition of the Mishnah-rule is complete. We now turn to a systematic Aggadic composition on the theme of the Halakhah. I have supplied sub-heads to clarify the movement of topics.

A Theology of Gentile Idolatry: Its Origins and its Implications for Holy Israel

I.2 A. R. Hanina bar Pappa, and some say, R. Simlai, gave the following exposition [of the verse, "They that fashion a graven image are all of them vanity, and their delectable things shall not profit, and their own witnesses see not nor know" (Isa. 44:9)]: "In the age to come the Holy One, blessed be He, will bring a scroll of the Torah and hold it in his bosom and say, 'Let him who has kept himself busy with it come and take his reward.' Then all the gentiles will crowd together: 'All of the nations are gathered together' (Isa. 43:9). The Holy One, blessed be He, will say to them, 'Do not crowd together before me in a mob. But let each nation enter together with [2B] its scribes, 'and let the peoples be gathered together' (Isa. 43:9), and the word 'people' means 'kingdom': 'and one kingdom shall be stronger than the other' (Gen. 25:23)."

B. *But can there be a mob scene before the Holy One, blessed be He? Rather, it is so that from their perspective they not form a mob, so that they will be able to hear what he says to them.*

C. [Resuming the narrative of A:] "The kingdom of Rome comes in first."

D. *How come? Because they are the most important. How do we know on the basis of Scripture they are the most important? Because it is written, "And he shall devour the whole earth and shall tread it down and break it into pieces" (Gen. 25:23), and said R. Yohanan, "This Rome is answerable, for its definition [of matters] has gone forth to the entire world [Mishcon: 'this refers to Rome, whose power is known to the whole world']."*

E. *And how do we know that the one who is most important comes in first? It is in accord with that which R. Hisda said.*

F. For said R. Hisda, "When the king and the community [await judgment], the king enters in first for judgment: 'That he maintain the case of his servant [Solomon] and [then] the cause of his people Israel' (1 Kgs. 8:59)."

G. *And how come? If you wish, I shall say it is not appropriate to keep the king sitting outside. And if you wish, I shall say that [the king is allowed to plea his case] before the anger of the Holy One is aroused.*

H. [Resuming the narrative of C:] "The Holy One, blessed be He, will say to them, 'How have you defined your chief occupation?'
I. "They will say before him, 'Lord of the world, a vast number of marketplaces have we set up, a vast number of bathhouses we have made, a vast amount of silver and gold have we accumulated. And all of these things we have done only in behalf of Israel, so that they may define as their chief occupation the study of the Torah.'
J. "The Holy One, blessed be He, will say to them, 'You complete idiots! Whatever you have done has been for your own convenience. You have set up a vast number of marketplaces to be sure, but that was so as to set up whorehouses in them. The bathhouses were for your own pleasure. Silver and gold belong to me anyhow: "Mine is the silver and mine is the gold, says the Lord of hosts" (Hag. 2:8). Are there any among you who have been telling of "this," and "this" is only the Torah: "And this is the Torah that Moses set before the children of Israel' (Deut. 4:44)." So they will make their exit, humiliated.
K. "When the kingdom of Rome has made its exit, the kingdom of Persia enters afterward."
   L. *How come? Because they are second in importance. And how do we know it on the basis of Scripture? Because it is written,* "And behold, another beast, a second, like a bear" (Dan. 7:5), *and in this connection R. Joseph repeated as a Tannaite formulation,* "This refers to the Persians, who eat and drink like a bear, are obese like a bear, are shaggy like a bear, and are restless like a bear."
M. "The Holy One, blessed be He, will say to them, 'How have you defined your chief occupation?'
N. "They will say before him, 'Lord of the world, We have thrown up a vast number of bridges, we have conquered a vast number of towns, we have made a vast number of wars, and all of them we did only for Israel, so that they may define as their chief occupation the study of the Torah.'
O. "The Holy One, blessed be He, will say to them, 'Whatever you have done has been for your own convenience. You have thrown up a vast number of bridges, to collect tolls, you have conquered a vast number of towns, to collect the corvée, and, as to making a vast number of wars, I am the one who makes wars: "The Lord is a man of war" (Ex. 19:17). Are there any among you who have been telling of "this," and "this" is only the Torah: "And this is the Torah that Moses set before the children of Israel" (Deut. 4:44).' So they will make their exit, humiliated.
   P. *But if the kingdom of Persia has seen that such a claim issued by the kingdom of Rome did no good whatsoever, how come they go in at all?*
   Q. *They will say to themselves,* "These are the ones who destroyed the house of the sanctuary, but we are the ones who built it."

3. The Talmud's Union of Halakhah and Aggadah... 43

R. "And so it will go with each and every nation."
  S. *But if each one of them has seen that such a claim issued by the others did no good whatsoever, how come they go in at all?*
  T. *They will say to themselves, "Those two subjugated Israel, but we never subjugated Israel."*
  U. *And how come the two conquering nations are singled out as important and the others are not?*
  V. *It is because the rule of these will continue until the Messiah comes.*
W. "They will say to him, 'Lord of the world, in point of fact, did you actually give it to us and we did not accept it?'"
  X. *But how can they present such an argument, since it is written,* "The Lord came from Sinai and rose from Seir to them, he shined forth from Mount Paran" (Deut. 33:2), *and further,* "God comes from Teman" (Hab. 3:3). *Now what in the world did he want in Seir, and what was he looking for in Paran?* Said R. Yohanan, "This teaches that the Holy One, blessed be He, made the rounds of each and every nation and language and none accepted it, until he came to Israel, and they accepted it."
  Y. *Rather, this is what they say,* "Did we accept it but then not carry it out?"
  Z. *But to this the rejoinder must be,* "Why did you not accept it anyhow!"
AA. Rather, "this is what they say before him, 'Lord of the world, did you hold a mountain over us like a cask and then we refused to accept it as you did to Israel, as it is written, "And they stood beneath the mountain" (Ex. 19:17).'"
  BB. And [in connection with the verse, "And they stood beneath the mountain" (Ex. 19:17),] said R. Dimi bar Hama, "This teaches that the Holy One, blessed be He, held the mountain over Israel like a cask and said to them, 'If you accept the Torah, well and good, and if not, then there is where your grave will be.'"
CC. "Then the Holy One, blessed be He, will say to them, 'Let us make known what happened first: "Let them announce to us former things" (Isa. 43:9). As to the seven religious duties that you did accept, where have you actually carried them out?'"
  DD. *And how do we know on the basis of Scripture that they did not carry them out? R. Joseph formulated as a Tannaite statement,* "'He stands and shakes the earth, he sees and makes the nations tremble' (Hab. 3:6): what did he see? He saw the seven religious duties that the children of Noah accepted upon themselves as obligations but never actually carried them out. Since they did not carry out those obligations, he went and remitted their obligation."

EE. *But then they benefited — so it pays to sin!*

FF. Said Mar b. Rabina, [3A] "What this really proves is that even when they carry out those religious duties, they get no reward on that account."

GG. *And they don't, don't they? But has it not been taught on Tannaite authority:* R. Meir would say, "How on the basis of Scripture do we know that, even if it is a gentile, if he goes and takes up the study of the Torah as his occupation, he is equivalent to the high priest? Scripture states, 'You shall therefore keep my statutes and my ordinances, which, if a human being does them, one shall gain life through them' (Lev. 18:5). What is written is not 'priests' or 'Levites' or 'Israelites,' but rather, 'a human being.' So you have learned the fact that, even if it is a gentile, if he goes and takes up the study of the Torah as his occupation, he is equivalent to the high priest."

HH. Rather, what you learn from this [DD] is that they will not receive that reward that is coming to those who are commanded to do them and who carry them out, but rather, the reward that they receive will be like that coming to the one who is not commanded to do them and who carries them out anyhow.

II. For said R. Hanina, "Greater is the one who is commanded and who carries out the religious obligations than the one who is not commanded but nonetheless carries out religious obligations."

JJ. [Reverting to AA, CC:] "This is what the gentiles say before him, 'Lord of the world, Israel, who accepted it — where in the world have they actually carried it out?'

KK. "The Holy One, blessed be He, will say to them, 'I shall bear witness concerning them, that they have carried out the whole of the Torah!'

LL. "They will say before him, 'Lord of the world, is there a father who is permitted to give testimony concerning his son? For it is written, "Israel is my son, my firstborn" (Ex. 4:22).'

MM. "The Holy One, blessed be He, will say to them, 'The Heaven and the earth will give testimony in their behalf that they have carried out the entirety of the Torah.'

NN. "They will say before him, 'Lord of the world, the Heaven and earth have a selfish interest in the testimony that they give: 'If not for my covenant with day and with night, I should not have appointed the ordinances of Heaven and earth' (Jer. 33:25).'"

OO. *For said R. Simeon b. Laqish, "What is the meaning of the verse of Scripture,* 'And there was evening, and there was morning, the sixth day' (Gen. 1:31)? This teaches that the Holy One, blessed be He, made a stipulation with all of the works of creation, saying to them, 'If Israel accepts my Torah, well and good, but if not, I shall return you to chaos and

3. The Talmud's Union of Halakhah and Aggadah... 45

void.' *That is in line with what is written:* 'You did cause sentence to be heard from Heaven, the earth trembled and was still' (Ps. 76:9). If 'trembling,' then where is the stillness, and if 'stillness,' then where is the trembling? Rather, to begin with, trembling, but at the end, stillness."

PP. [Reverting to MM-NN:] "The Holy One, blessed be He, will say to them, 'Some of them may well come and give testimony concerning Israel that they have observed the entirety of the Torah. Let Nimrod come and give testimony in behalf of Abraham that he never worshipped idols. Let Laban come and give testimony in behalf of Jacob, that he never was suspect of thievery. Let the wife of Potiphar come and give testimony in behalf of Joseph, that he was never suspect of 'sin.' Let Nebuchadnessar come and give testimony in behalf of Hananiah, Mishael, and Azariah, that they never bowed down to the idol. Let Darius come and give testimony in behalf of Daniel, that he did not neglect even the optional prayers. Let Bildad the Shuhite and Zophar the Naamatite and Eliphaz the Temanite and Elihu son of Barachel the Buzite come and testify in behalf of Israel that they have observed the entirety of the Torah: "Let the nations bring their own witnesses, that they may be justified" (Isa. 43:9).'

QQ. "They will say before him, 'Lord of the world, Give it to us to begin with, and let us carry it out.'

RR. "The Holy One, blessed be He, will say to them, 'World-class idiots! He who took the trouble to prepare on the eve of the Sabbath [Friday] will eat on the Sabbath, but he who took no trouble on the even of the Sabbath — what in the world is he going to eat on the Sabbath! Still, [I'll give you another chance.] I have a rather simple religious duty, which is called "the tabernacle." Go and do that one.'"

SS. *But can you say any such thing? Lo, R. Joshua b. Levi has said, "What is the meaning of the verse of Scripture,* 'The ordinances that I command you this day to do them' (Deut. 7:11)? Today is the day to do them, but not tomorrow; they are not to be done tomorrow; today is the day to do them, but not the day on which to receive a reward for doing them."

TT. Rather, it is that the Holy One, blessed be He, does not exercise tyranny over his creatures.

UU. *And why does he refer to it as a simple religious duty? Because it does not involve enormous expense [to carry out that religious duty].*

VV. "Forthwith every one of them will take up the task and go and make a tabernacle on his roof. But then the Holy, One, blessed be He, will come and make the sun blaze over them as at the summer solstice, and every one of them will knock down his tabernacle and go his way: 'Let us break their bands asunder and cast away their cords from us' (Ps. 23:3)."

WW. But lo, you have just said, "it is that the Holy One, blessed be He, does not exercise tyranny over his creatures"!

XX. *It is because the Israelites, too — sometimes* **[3B]** *the summer solstice goes on to the festival of Tabernacles, and therefore they are bothered by the heat!*

YY. But has not Raba stated, "One who is bothered [by the heat] is exempt from the obligation of dwelling in the tabernacle"?

ZZ. *Granting that one may be exempt from the duty, is he going to go and tear the thing down?*

AAA. "Then the Holy One, blessed be He, goes into session and laughs at them: 'He who sits in Heaven laughs' (Ps. 2:4)."

BBB. Said R. Isaac, "Laughter before the Holy One, blessed be He, takes place only on that day alone."

CCC. *There are those who repeat as a Tannaite version this statement of R. Isaac in respect to that which has been taught on Tannaite authority:*

DDD. R. Yosé says, "In the coming age gentiles will come and convert."

EEE. *But will they be accepted? Has it not been taught on Tannaite authority:* Converts will not be accepted in the days of the Messiah, just as they did not accept proselytes either in the time of David or in the time of Solomon?

FFF. Rather, "they will make themselves appear to be converts, and they will put on phylacteries on their heads and arms and fringes on their garments and a mezuzah on their doors. But when they witness the war of Gog and Magog, he will say to them, 'How come you have come?' They will say, '"Against the Lord and against his Messiah."' For so it is said, 'Why are the nations in an uproar and why do the peoples mutter in vain' (Ps. 2:1). Then each one of them will rid himself of his religious duty and go his way: 'Let us break their bands asunder' (Ps. 2:3). Then the Holy One, blessed be He, goes into session and laughs at them: 'He who sits in Heaven laughs' (Ps. 2:4)."

GGG Said R. Isaac, "Laughter before the Holy One, blessed be He, takes place only on that day alone."

HHH. But is this really so? And has not R. Judah said Rab said, "The day is made up of twelve hours. In the first three the Holy One, blessed be He, goes into session and engages in study of the Torah; in the second he goes into session and judges the entire world. When he realizes that the world is liable to annihilation, he arises from the throne of justice and takes up a seat on the throne of mercy. In the third period he goes into session and nourishes the whole

3. The Talmud's Union of Halakhah and Aggadah...   47

world from the horned buffalo to the brood of vermin. During the fourth quarter he laughs [and plays] with leviathan: 'There is leviathan, whom you have formed to play with' (Ps. 104:26)." [This proves that God does laugh more than on that one day alone.]

III. Said R. Nahman bar Isaac, "With his creatures he laughs [every day], but at his creatures he laughs only on that day alone."

I.3 A. Said R. Aha to R. Nahman bar Isaac, "From the day on which the house of the sanctuary, the Holy One blessed be He has had no laughter.

B. *"And how on the basis of Scripture do we know that he has had none? If we say that it is because it is written,* 'And on that day did the Lord, the god of hosts, call to weeping and lamentation' (Isa. 22:12), *that verse refers to that day in particular. Shall we then say that that fact derives from the verse,* 'If I forget you, Jerusalem, let my right hand forget her cunning, let my tongue cleave to the roof of my mouth if I do not remember you' (Ps. 137:5-6)? *That refers to forgetfulness, not laughter. Rather, the fact derives from this verse:* 'I have long held my peace, I have been still, I have kept in, now I will cry' (Isa. 42:14)."

I.4 A. [Referring to the statement that during the fourth quarter he laughs [and plays] with leviathan,] *[nowadays] what does he do in the fourth quarter of the day?*

B. He sits and teaches Torah to kindergarten students: "Whom shall one teach knowledge, and whom shall one make understand the message? Those who are weaned from the milk? (Isa. 28:19).

C. *And to begin with [prior to the destruction of the Temple, which ended his spending his time playing with leviathan], who taught them?*

D. *If you wish, I shall say it was Metatron, and if you wish, I shall say that he did both [but now does only one].*

E. And at night what does he do?

F. *If you wish, I shall say that it is the sort of thing he does by day;*

G. *and if you wish, I shall say,* he rides his light cherub and floats through eighteen thousand worlds: "The chariots of God are myriads, even thousands and thousands [*shinan*] (Ps. 68:17). Read the letters translated as thousands, *shinan,* as though they were written, *she-enan,* meaning, that are not [thus: "the chariots are twice ten thousand less two thousand, eighteen thousand (Mishcon)].

H. *And if you wish, I shall say,* he sits and listens to the song of the Living Creatures [*hayyot*]: "By the day the Lord will command his loving kindness and in the night his song shall be with me" (Ps. 42:9).

The negative case, the indictment of the gentiles, is now complete. What is required is an affirmative case for the election of Israel, and that depends entirely on Israel's devotion to the Torah.

THE CRITICAL IMPORTANCE OF TORAH-STUDY FOR THE SALVATION OF ISRAEL, INDIVIDUALLY AND COLLECTIVELY

I.5 A. Said R. Levi, "To whoever stops studying the words of the Torah and instead takes up words of mere chatter they feed glowing coals of juniper: 'They pluck salt-wort with wormwood and the roots of juniper are their food' (Job 30:4)."

B. Said R. Simeon b. Laqish, "For whoever engages in study of the Torah by night — the Holy One, blessed be He, draws out the thread of grace by day: 'By day the Lord will command his loving kindness, and in the night his song shall be with me' (Ps. 42:9). Why is it that 'By day the Lord will command his loving kindness'? Because 'in the night his song shall be with me.'"

C. *Some say,* said R. Simeon b. Laqish, "For whoever engages in study of the Torah in this world, which is like the night, — the Holy One, blessed be He, draws out the thread of grace in the world to come, which is like the day: 'By day the Lord will command his loving kindness, and in the night his song shall be with me' (Ps. 42:9). [Supply: Why is it that 'By day the Lord will command his loving kindness'? Because 'in the night his song shall be with me.']"

I.6 A. Said R. Judah said Samuel, *"What is the meaning of the verse of Scripture,* 'And you make man as the fish of the sea and as the creeping things, that have no ruler over them' (Hab. 1:14)? Why are human beings compared to fish of the sea? To tell you, just as fish in the sea, when they come up on dry land, forthwith begin to die, so with human beings, when they take their leave of teachings of the Torah and religious deeds, forthwith they begin to die.

B. "Another matter: just as the fish of the sea, as soon as dried by the sun, die, so human beings, when struck by the sun, die."

C. *If you want, this refers to this world, and if you want, this refers to the world to come.*

D. *If you want, this refers to this world, in line with that which R. Hanina [said],* for said R. Hanina, "Everything is in the hands of Heaven except cold and heat: 'colds and heat boils are in the way of the froward, he who keeps his soul holds himself far from them' (Prov. 22:5)."

E. *And if you want, this refers to the world to come, in accord with that which was stated by R. Simeon b. Laqish.* For said R. Simeon b. Laqish, "In the world to come, there is no Gehenna, but rather, the Holy One, blessed be He, brings the sun out of its sheathe and he heats the wicked but heals the righteous through it. The wicked are brought to judgment by [4A] it: 'For behold, the day comes, it burns as a furnace, and all the proud and all who do wicked things shall be stubble, and the day that comes shall set them ablaze, says the Lord of hosts, that it shall leave them neither root nor branch' (Mal. 3:19).

F. "'It shall leave them neither root' — in this world; 'nor branch' — in the world to come.

G. "'but heals the righteous through it': 'But to you that fear my name shall the sun of righteousness arise with healing in its wings' (Mal. 3:19). They will revel in it: 'And you shall go forth and gambol as calves of the stall' (Mal. 3:20)."

H. [Continuing B, above:] "Another matter: just as with the fish of the sea, whoever is bigger than his fellow swallows his fellow, so in the case of human beings, were it not for fear of the government, whoever is bigger than his fellow would swallow his fellow."

I. *That is in line with what we have learned in the Mishnah:* **R. Hananiah, Prefect of the Priests, says, "Pray for the welfare of the government. For if it were not for fear of it, one man would swallow his fellow alive"** [M. Abot 3:2A-B].

Now the two propositions are joined and formed into an eschatological doctrine: where are matters heading? Is idolatry permanent, the estrangement of God and the gentiles eternal? The answer is, matters are heading toward a resolution at the end of days, when God will destroy idolatry and endow Israel with eternal life.

GOD FAVORS HOLY ISRAEL OVER THE GENTILES, BECAUSE THE FORMER ACCEPT, STUDY, AND CARRY OUT THE TORAH AND THE LATTER DO NOT. THEREFORE AT THE END OF DAYS GOD WILL SAVE ISRAEL AND DESTROY IDOLATRY

I.7 A. R. Hinena bar Pappa contrasted verses of Scripture: "It is written, 'As to the almighty, we do not find him exercising plenteous power' (Job 37:23), but by contrast, 'Great is our Lord and of abundant power' (Ps. 147:5), and further, 'Your right hand, Lord, is glorious in power' (Ex. 15:6).

B. "But there is no contradiction between the first and second and third statements, for the former speaks of the time of judgment [when justice is tempered with mercy, so God does not do what he could] and the latter two statements refer to a time of war [of God against his enemies]."

I.8 A. R. Hama bar Hanina contrasted verses of Scripture: "It is written, 'Fury is not in me' (Isa. 27:4) but also 'The Lord revenges and is furious' (Nah. 1:2).

B. *"But there is no contradiction between the first and second statements,* for the former speaks of Israel, the latter of the gentiles."

C. R. Hinena bar Pappa said, "'Fury is not in me' (Isa. 27:4), for I have already taken an oath: 'would that I had not so vowed, then as the briars and thorns in flame would I with one step burn it altogether.'"

I.9 A. *That is in line with what R. Alexandri said, "What is the meaning of the verse,* 'And it shall come to pass on that day that I will seek to destroy all the nations' (Zech. 12:9) —

B. "'Seek' — seek permission from whom?

C. "Said the Holy One, blessed be He, 'I shall seek in the records that deal with them, to see whether there is a cause of merit, on account of which I shall redeem them, but if not, I shall destroy them.'"

I.10 A. *That is in line with what Raba said, "What is the meaning of the verse,* 'Howbeit he will not stretch out a hand for a ruinous heap though they cry in his destruction' (Job 30:24)?

B. "Said the Holy One, blessed be He, to Israel, 'When I judge Israel, I shall not judge them as I do the gentiles, for it is written, "I will overturn, overturn, overturn it" (Ezek. 21:32), rather, I shall exact punishment from them as a hen pecks.'

C. "Another matter: 'Even if the Israelites do not carry out a religious duty before me more than a hen pecking at a rubbish heap, I shall join together [all the little pecks] into a great sum: "although they pick little they are saved" (Job 30:24) [following Mishcon's rendering].'

D. "Another matter: 'As a reward for their crying out to me, I shall help them' (Job 30:24) [following Mishcon's rendering]."

I.11 A. *That is in line with what R. Abba said, "What is the meaning of the verse,* 'Though I would redeem them, yet they have spoken

3. The Talmud's Union of Halakhah and Aggadah...

lies against me' (Hos. 7:23)? 'I said that I would redeem them through [inflicting a penalty] on their property in this world, so that they might have the merit of enjoying the world to come, "yet they have spoken lies against me" (Hos. 7:23).'"

I.12 A. *That is in line with what R. Pappi in the name of Raba said, "What is the meaning of the verse,* 'Though I have trained [and] strengthened their arms, yet they imagine mischief against me' (Hos. 7:15)?

B. Said the Holy One, blessed be He, I thought that I would punish them with suffering in this world, so that their arm might be strengthened in the world to come, "yet they have spoken lies against me" (Hos. 7:23).'"

God's own traits now enter in. Is God wrathful or merciful? The answer is, God is merciful and forgives.

GOD'S JUDGMENT AND WRATH, GOD'S MERCY AND FORGIVENESS

I.13 A. *R. Abbahu praised R. Safra to the* minim [in context: Christian authorities of Caesarea], *saying that he was a highly accomplished authority. They therefore remitted his taxes for thirteen years.*

B. *One day they came upon him and said to him,* "It is written, 'You only have I known among all the families of the earth; therefore I will visit upon you all your iniquities' (Amos 3:2). *If one is angry, does he vent it on someone he loves?"*

C. *He fell silent and said nothing at all. They wrapped a scarf around his neck and tortured him. R. Abbahu came along and found them. He said to them, "Why are you torturing him?"*

D. *They said to him, "Didn't you tell us that he is* a highly accomplished authority, *but he does not know how to explain this verse!"*

E. *He said to them, "True enough, I told you that he was a master of Tannaite statements, but did I say anything at all to you about his knowledge of Scripture?"*

F. *They said to him, "So how come you know?"*

G. *He said to them, "Since we, for our part, spend a lot of time with you, we have taken the task of studying it thoroughly, while others [in Babylonia, Safra's place of origin] do not study [Scripture] that carefully."*

H. *They said to him, "So tell us."*

I. He said to them, "I shall tell you a parable. To what is the matter comparable? To the case of a man who lent money to two people, one a friend, the other an enemy. From the friend he collects the money little by little, from the enemy he collects all at once."

I.14 A. Said R. Abba bar Kahana, "What is the meaning of the following verse of Scripture: 'Far be it from you to do after this manner, to slay the righteous with the wicked' (Gen. 18:25).

B. "Said Abraham before the Holy One, blessed be He, 'Lord of the world! It is a profanation to act in such a way [a play on the Hebrew letters, shared by the words 'far be it' and 'profanation'], 'to slay the righteous with the wicked' (Gen. 18:25)."
C. But is it not [so that God might do just that]? And is it not written, "And I will cut off from you the righteous and the wicked" (Ezek. 21:8)?
D. That speaks of one who is not completely righteous, but not of one who is completely righteous.
E. And will he not do so to one who is completely righteous? And is it not written, "And begin the slaughter with my sanctuary" (Ezek. 9:6), in which connection R. Joseph repeated as a Tannaite version, "Read not 'with my sanctuary' but rather, 'with those who are holy to me,' namely, the ones who carried out the Torah beginning to end."
F. *There, too,* since they had the power to protest against the wickedness of the others and did not do so, they were not regarded as completely righteous at all.

I.15 A. *R. Pappa contrasted verses of Scripture:* "It is written, 'God is angry every day' (Ps. 7:12) but also 'who could stand before his anger' (Nah. 1:6).
B. *"But there is no contradiction between the first and second statements,* for the former speaks of the individual, the latter of the community."

The reference to the Minim, in this context, Christians, raises the subject of the prophet to the gentiles, Balaam, who stands in for Jesus in the religious polemic constructed by the Aggadic masters.

BALAAM, THE PROPHET OF THE GENTILES, AND ISRAEL; GOD'S ANGER WITH THE GENTILES AND WITH ISRAEL

I.16 A. *Our rabbis have taught on Tannaite authority:*
B. "God is angry every day" (Ps. 7:12), and how long is his anger? It is for a moment. And how long is a moment? The portion 1/53,848th of an hour is a moment.
C. And no creature can determine that moment, except for Balaam that wicked man, of whom it is written, [4B] "who knew the knowledge of the Most High" (Num. 24:16).
D. How can it be that a man who did not know the mind of his animal could have known the mind of the Most High?

I.17 A. *And what is the meaning of the statement that* he did not know the mind of his animal?
B. *When they saw him riding on his ass, they said to him, "How come you're not riding on a horse?"*
C. *He said to them, "I sent it to the meadow."*

3. The Talmud's Union of Halakhah and Aggadah... 53

    D. Forthwith: "The ass said, Am I not your ass" (Num. 22:30).
    E. *He said to it, "Just as a beast of burden in general."*
    F. *She said to him,* "Upon whom you have ridden" (Num. 22:30).
    G. *He said to it, "Only from time to time."*
    H. *She said to him,* "ever since I was yours (Num. 22:30). And not only so, but I serve you for riding by day and fucking by night."
    I. For here the word "I was wont" is used, and the same letters bear the meaning of bed-mate: "...and she served him as a bed-mate" (1 Kgs. 1:2).

I.18 A. *And what is the meaning of the statement that* he could have known the mind of the Most High?
    B. For he knew precisely that moment at which the Holy One, blessed be He, was angry.
    C. *That is in line with what the prophet had said to them,* "O my people, remember now what Balak king of Moab consulted and what Balaam son of Beor answered him from Shittim to Gilgal, that you may know the righteousness of the Lord" (Mic. 6:5).

I.19 A. ["O my people, remember now what Balak king of Moab consulted and what Balaam son of Beor answered him from Shittim to Gilgal, that you may know the righteousness of the Lord" (Mic. 6:5)]:
    B. Said R. Eleazar, "Said R. Eleazar, "Said the Holy One, blessed be He, to Israel, 'My people, see how many acts of righteousness I carried out with you, for I did not grow angry with you during all those [perilous] days, for if I had grown angry with you, there would not have remained from Israel a remnant or a survivor.'
    C. "And that is in line with what Balaam says: 'How can I curse seeing that God does not curse, and how can I be wrathful, seeing that the Lord has not been wrathful' (Num. 23:8)."

I.20 A. And how long is his wrath? It is for a moment. And how long is a moment? The portion 1/53,848th of an hour is a moment.
    B. And how long is a moment?
    C. Said Amemar — others say, Rabina — "So long as it takes to say the word 'moment.'"
    D. *And how on the basis of Scripture do we know that his wrath lasts for only a moment?*
    E. *As it is written,* "For his anger is for a moment, his favor is for a lifetime" (Ps. 30:6).
    F. *If you prefer:* "Hide yourself for a brief moment, until the wrath be past" (Isa. 26:20).

I.21 A. *When is he angry?*
    B. *Said Abbayye, "In the first three hours of the day, when the comb of the cock is white."*
    C. *Isn't it white all the rest of the day?*
    D. *At other times it has red streaks, but then it has none.*

I.22 A. R. Joshua b. Levi — a certain Min would bother him about verses of Scripture. Once he took a chicken and put it between the legs of the bed and watched it. He reasoned, "When that hour comes, I shall curse him."

B. But when that hour came, he was dozing. He said, "What you learn from this experience is that it is not correct to act in such a way: 'His tender mercies are over all his works' (Ps. 145:9), 'Neither is it good for the righteous to inflict punishment' (Prov. 17:26)."

THE TIME OF GOD'S ANGER IN RELATIONSHIP TO THE GENTILES AND TO ISRAEL; THE ROLE OF IDOLATRY IN GOD'S WRATH AGAINST THE NATIONS

I.23 A. *It was taught as a Tannaite version in the name of R. Meir,* "[That time at which God gets angry comes] when the kings put on their crowns on their heads and prostrate themselves to the sun. Forthwith the Holy One, blessed be He, grows angry."

I.24 A. *Said R. Joseph,* "A person should not recite the Prayer of the Additional Service for the first day of the New Year [the Day of Judgment] during the first three hours of the day or in private, lest, since that is the time of judgment, his deeds may be examined, and his prayer rejected."

B. *If so, then the prayer of the community also should not be recited at that time?*

C. The merit [accruing to the community as a whole] is greater.

D. *If so, then that of the Morning Service also should not be recited in private?*

E. Since at that time the community also will be engaged in reciting the Morning Prayer, the individual's recitation of the Prayer will not be rejected.

F. *But have you not said,* "In the first three the Holy One, blessed be He, goes into session and engages in study of the Torah; in the second he goes into session and judges the entire world"?

G. *Reverse the order.*

H. *Or, if you prefer, actually do not reverse the order.* For when God is occupied with study of the Torah, called by Scripture "truth" as in "buy the truth and do not sell it" (Prov. 23:23), the Holy One, blessed be He, in any event will not violate the strict rule of justice. But when engaged in judgment, which is not called "truth" by Scripture, the Holy One, blessed be He, may step across the line of strict justice [towards mercy].

I.25 A. Reverting to the body of the prior text:

B. *R. Joshua b. Levi has said,* "What is the meaning of the verse of Scripture, 'The ordinances that I command you this day to do them' (Deut. 7:11)? Today is the day to do them, but not tomorrow; they are not to be done

3. The Talmud's Union of Halakhah and Aggadah...   55

tomorrow; today is the day to do them, but today is not the day on which to receive a reward for doing them":

C. Said R. Joshua b. Levi, "All the religious duties that Israelites do in this world come and give evidence in their behalf in the world to come: 'Let them bring their witnesses that they may be justified, let them hear and say it is truth.'"

D. "Let them bring their witnesses that they may be justified": this is Israel.

E. "Let them hear and say it is truth": this refers to the gentiles.

F. And said R. Joshua b. Levi, "All the religious duties that Israelites do in this world come and flap about the faces of gentiles in the world to come: 'Keep them and do them, for this, your wisdom and understanding, will be in the eyes of the peoples' (Deut. 4:6).

G. "What is stated here is not 'in the presence of the peoples' but 'in the eyes of the peoples,' which teaches you that they will come and flap about the faces of gentiles in the world to come."

H. And said R. Joshua b. Levi, "The Israelites made the golden calf only to give an opening to penitents: 'O that they had such a heart as this always, to fear me and keep my commandments' (Deut. 5:26)."

The Messiah-theme has arisen and is pursued in its own terms.

THE SINFUL ANCESTOR OF THE MESSIAH AND GOD'S FORGIVENESS OF HIM AND OF ISRAEL

I.26 A. That is in line with what R. Yohanan said in the name of R. Simeon b. Yohai: "David was really not so unfit as to do such a deed [as he did with Beth Sheva]: 'My heart is slain within me' (Ps. 109:22) [Mishcon: David's inclinations had been completely conquered by himself]. And the Israelites were hardly the kind of people to commit such an act: "O that they had such a heart as this always, to fear me and keep my commandments' (Deut. 5:26). So why did they do it?

B. "[5A] It was to show you that if an individual has sinned, they say to him, 'Go to the individual [such as David, and follow his example], and if the community as a whole has sinned, they say to them, 'Go to the community [such as Israel].'

C. *And it was necessary to give both examples. For had we been given the rule governing the individual, that might have been supposed to be because his personal sins were not broadly known, but in the case of the community, the sins of which* will be broadly known, I might have said that that is not the case.

D. And if we had been given the rule governing the community, that might have been supposed to be the case because they enjoy greater mercy, but an individual, who has not got such powerful zekhut, might have been thought not subject to the rule.

E. So both cases had to be made explicit.

I.27 A. That is in line with what R. Samuel bar Nahmani said R. Jonathan said, "What is the meaning of the verse of Scripture, 'The saying of David, son of Jesse, and the saying of the man raised on high' (2 Sam. 23:1)?

B. "It means, 'The saying of David, son of Jesse, the man who raised up the yoke of repentance.'"

I.28 A. Said R. Samuel bar Nahmani said R. Jonathan, "Whoever does a religious duty in this world — that deed goes before him to the world to come, as it is said, 'And your righteousness shall go before you' (Isa. 58:8).

B. "And whoever commits a transgression in this world — that act turns aside from him and goes before him on the Day of Judgment, as it is said, 'The paths of their way are turned aside, they go up into the waste and perish' (Job 6:18)."

C. R. Eliezer says, "It attaches to him like a dog, as it is said, 'He did not listen to her to lie by her or to be with her' (Gen. 39:10).

D. "'To lie by her' in this world.

E. "'Or to be with her' in the world to come."

I.29 A. Said R. Simeon b. Laqish, "Come and let us express our gratitude to our ancestors, for if it were not for their having sinned, we for our part should never have been able to come into the world: 'I said you are gods and all of you sons of the Most High' (Ps. 82:6). Now that you have ruined things by what you have done, 'you shall indeed die like mortals' (Ps. 82:6)."

B. *Does that statement then bear the implication, therefore, that if they had not sinned, they would not have propagated? But has it not been written,* "And you, be fruitful and multiply" (Gen. 9:7)?

C. *That applies up to Sinai.*

D. *But in connection with Sinai it also is written,* "Go say to them, Go back to your tents" (Ex. 19:15), *meaning, to marital relationships. And is it not also written,* "that it might be well with them and with their children" (Deut. 5:26)?

E. That speaks only to those who were actually present at Mount Sinai.

F. *But has not R. Simeon b. Laqish stated,* "What is the meaning of that which is written: 'This is the book of the generations of Adam' (Gen. 5:1)? Now did the first Adam have a book? The statement, rather, teaches that the Holy One, blessed be

3. The Talmud's Union of Halakhah and Aggadah... 57

He, showed to the first Adam each generation and its authoritative expositors, each generation and its sages, each generation and those that administered its affairs. When he came to the generation of R. Aqiba, he rejoiced in the master's Torah but he was saddened by the master's death.

G. "He said, 'How precious are your thoughts to me, O God' (Ps. 139:17)."

H. And said R. Yosé, "The son of David will come only when all of the souls that are stored up in the body will be used up: 'For I will not contend for ever, neither will I be always angry, for the spirit should fall before me and the spirits which I have made' (Isa. 57:16)." [Mishcon: In the face of the foregoing teachings, how could it be stated that had it not been for the sin of the golden calf, we should not have come into the world?]

I. *Do not, therefore, imagine that the sense of the statement is,* we should have not come into the world [if our ancestors had not sinned], *but rather, it would have been as though we had not come into the world.*

J. *Does that then bear the implication that, if they had not sinned, they would never have died? But have not the passages been written that deal with the deceased childless brother's widow and the chapters about inheritances [which take for granted that people die]?*

K. *These passages are written conditionally [meaning, if people sin and so die, then the rules take effect, but it is not necessary that they take effect unless that stipulation is fulfilled].*

L. *And are there then any verses of Scripture that are stated conditionally?*

M. *Indeed so, for said R. Simeon b. Laqish, "What is the meaning of that which has been written,* 'And it was evening and it was morning, the sixth day' (Gen. 1:31)? This teaches that the Holy One, blessed be He, made a stipulation with the works of creation and said, 'If the Israelites accept the Torah, well and good, but if not, I shall send you back to the condition of formlessness and void.'"

N. *An objection was raised:* "O that they had such a heart as this always, to fear me and keep my commandments, that it may be well with them and their children" (Deut. 5:26): it is not possible to maintain that the meaning here is that he would take away the angel of death from them, for the decree had already been made. It means that the Israelites accepted the Torah only so that no nation or tongue would rule over them: "that it might be well with them and their children after them." [Mishcon: How could R. Simeon b. Laqish hold that but for the golden calf worship Israel would have enjoyed physical deathlessness?]

O. *[R. Simeon b. Laqish] made his statement in accord with the position of this Tannaite authority, for it has been taught on Tannaite authority:*

P. R. Yosé says, "The Israelites accepted the Torah only so that the angel of death should not have power over them: 'I said you are gods and all of you are sons of the Most High. Now that you have ruined things by what you have done 'you shall indeed die like mortals' (Ps. 82:6)."

Q. *But to R. Yosé also must be addressed the question, has it not been written, "O that they had such a heart as this always, to fear me and keep my commandments, that it may be well with them and their children" (Deut. 5:26)? Goodness is what is promised, but there still will be death!*

R. R. Yosé will say to you, "If there is no death, what greater goodness can there ever be?"

S. *And the other Tannaite authority — how does he read the phrase,* "You shall indeed die"?

T. *The sense of* "death" *here is* "poverty," for a master has said, "Four classifications of persons are equivalent to corpses, and these are they: the poor man, the blind man, the person afflicted with the skin disease [of Lev. 13], and the person who has no children.

U. "The poor man, as it is written: 'for all the men are dead who sought your life' (Ex. 4:19). *Now who were they? This refers to Dathan and Abiram, and they were certainly not then dead,* they had only lost all their money.

V. "The blind man, as it is written: 'He has made me dwell in darkness as those that have been long dead' (Lam. 3:6).

W. "The person afflicted with the skin disease, as it is written: 'Let her, I pray you, not be as one who is dead' (Num. 12:12).

X. "And the person who has no children, as it is written: 'Give me children or else I die' (Gen. 30:1)."

I.30 A. *Our rabbis have taught on Tannaite authority:*

B. "If you walk in my statutes" (Lev. 26:3) — the word "if" is used in the sense of supplication, as in the verse, O that my people would hearken to me, that Israel would walk in my ways...I should soon subdue their enemies" (Ps. 81:14-15); "O that you had listened to my commandments, then my peace would have been as a river, your seed also would have been as the sand" (Isa. 48:18).

I.31 A. *Our rabbis have taught on Tannaite authority:*

B. "O that they had such a heart as this always, to fear me and keep my commandments, that it may be well with them and their children" (Deut. 5:26).

3. The Talmud's Union of Halakhah and Aggadah... 59

C. Said Moses to the Israelites, "You are a bunch of ingrates, children of ingrates. When the Holy One, blessed be He, said to you, 'O that they had such a heart as this always, to fear me and keep my commandments, that it may be well with them and their children' (Deut. 5:26), they should have said, 'You give it.'

D. "They were ingrates, since it is written, 'Our soul loathes [5B] this light bread' (Num. 21:5).

E. "...the children of ingrates: 'The woman whom you gave to be with me, she gave me of the fruit of the tree and I ate it' (Gen. 3:12).

F. "So our rabbi, Moses, gave an indication of that fact to the Israelites only after forty years: 'And I have led you forty years in the wilderness...but the Lord has not give you a heart to know and eyes to see and ears to hear unto this day' (Deut. 29:3, 4)."

I.32 A. ["And I have led you forty years in the wilderness...but the Lord has not given you a heart to know and eyes to see and ears to hear unto this day" (Deut. 29:3, 4):]

B. Said Raba, "This proves that a person will fully grasp the mind of his master only after forty years have passed."

I.33 A. *Said R. Yohanan in the name of R. Benaah, "What is the meaning of the verse of Scripture,* 'Happy are you who sow beside all waters, that send forth the feet of the ox and the ass' (Isa. 32:20)? 'Happy are you, O Israel, when you are devoted to the Torah and to doing deeds of grace, then their inclination to do evil is handed over to them, and they are not handed over into the power of their inclination to do evil.

B. "For it is said, 'Happy are you who sow beside all waters.' For what does the word 'sowing' mean, if not 'doing deeds of grace,' in line with the use of the word in this verse: 'Sow for yourselves in righteousness, reap according to mercy' (Hos. 10:12), and what is the meaning of 'water' if not Torah: 'Oh you who are thirsty, come to the water' (Isa. 55:1)."

C. As to the phrase, "that send forth the feet of the ox and the ass":

D. it has been taught by the Tannaite authority of the household of Elijah:

E. "A person should always place upon himself the work of studying the Torah as an ox accepts the yoke, and as an ass, its burden."

III. FROM THE MISHNAH TO THE TALMUD, FROM THE HALAKHAH TO THE AGGADAH

The Mishnah's presentation of the Halakhah asks not a single question of history or theology. It deals only with commercial relationships with gentiles, so far as these are affected by idolatry, idols, and libation wine. So the topic at hand is treated in a routine and commonplace manner. The Talmud through its Aggadic composites transforms and transcends the Halakhic topic. It transforms it by reframing the issue of idolatry so that at stake is no longer relationships between

Israel and idolatrous nations but rather, those between idolatrous nations and God. It then transcends the topic by introducing the antidote to idolatry, which is the Torah. So Israel differs from idolatrous nations by reason of the Torah, and that imparts a special character to all of Israel's everyday conduct, not only its abstinence from idol-worship. In fact, the Talmud makes this tractate into an occasion for reflection on the problem of Israel and the nations.

Predictably, the Rabbinic sages invoke the one matter that they deem critical to all else: the Torah. Israel differs from the gentiles not for the merely negative reason that it does not worship idols but only an invisible God. It differs from them for the positive reason that the Torah that defines Israel's life was explicitly rejected by the gentiles. Every one of them had its chance at the Torah, and all of them rejected it. When the gentiles try to justify themselves to God by appealing to their forthcoming relationships to Israel, that is dismissed as self-serving. The gentiles could not even observe the seven commandments assigned to the Noahides, the children of humanity beyond the flood. From that point, the composite that stands at the head of the tractate and imparts its sense to all that will follow proceeds to the next question, that is, from the downfall of the gentiles by reason of their idolatry and rejection of the Torah to the salvation of Israel through the Torah.

Lest we miss the point, the reason for God's favor is made explicit: God favors Israel because Israel keeps the Torah. God therefore is strict with the gentiles but merciful to Israel. This is forthwith assigned a specific illustration: Balaam, the gentiles' prophet, presents the occasion to underscore God's anger toward the gentiles and his mercy to Israel. Bringing us back to the beginning, we then are shown how God's anger for the gentiles comes to the fore when the gentiles worship idols: when the kings who rule the world worship nature rather than nature's Creator. How God forgives Israel is then shown in respect to David's sin, and Torah-study as the antidote to sin once more is introduced. It is difficult to conclude other than that the framers of the Talmud have added to the presentation of the topic the results of profound thought on idolatry as a force in the history of humanity and of Israel. They thus have re-presented the Mishnah's topic in a far more profound framework of reflection than the Mishnah, with its rather petty interests in details of this and that, would have lead us to anticipate.

The next set of free-standing composites present episodic portraits of the matters introduced at the outset. The first involves world history and its periods, divided, it goes without saying, in relationship to the history of Israel, which stands at the center of world history. Rome defines the counterpart, and Israel's and Rome's relationships, culminating in the coming of the Messiah, are introduced. The next two collections form a point and counterpoint. On the one side, we have the tale of how Rabbi and the Roman Emperor formed a close relationship, with Rabbi the wise counselor, the ruler behind the throne. So whatever good happens in Rome happens by reason of our sages' wisdom, deriving as it does from the Torah, on which the stories predictably are going to harp. Then comes as explicit a judgment

3. The Talmud's Union of Halakhah and Aggadah...

upon Christianity in the framework of world-history as I think we are likely to find in the Talmud. And it is in that very context that the stories of Roman justice and Jewish martyrdom, by reason of Torah-study, are introduced. Not only so, but — should we miss the contrast the compilers wish to draw — the very same setting sets forth the counterpart and opposite: the stadium, circus, and theater, place for scoffers and buffoons, as against the sages' study-center, where people avoid the seat of the scornful but instead study the Torah.

The Talmud's associations with idolatry then compare and contrast these opposites: Israel vs. Rome; martyrdom vs. wantonness; Torah vs. lewdness and other forms of sin; probity and dignity and buffoonery; and on and on. The Mishnah's Halakhah finds no reason to introduce into the consideration of idolatry either the matter of the Torah or the issue of world history. The Talmud cannot deal with the details of conduct with gentiles without asking the profound questions of divine intentionality and human culpability that idolatry in the world provokes.

Now, we wonder, where have our sages learned to interpret the issue of idolatry in a theological framework, rather than in a merely practical and reasonable one, such as the Mishnah's authorship provides as the Halakhah? A glance at the verses of Scripture given earlier answers the question. Idolatry explains the fate of the nations, Israel's covenant through the Torah, Israel's. But the verses of Scripture cited earlier hardly serve as source for the reflections on Israel and Rome, the ages of human history, the power of God to forgive, and, above all, the glory of the Torah as the mediating source of God's love and forgiveness. All of this the Rabbinic sages themselves formulated and contributed. Scripture provided important data, the Mishnah, the Halakhic occasion, but for the theology of history formed around the center of the Torah, we look to the Aggadah for the occasion and the source.

IV. THEOLOGY IN THE CONTEXT OF THE LAW.
BAVLI ABODAH ZARAH 3:8A-C II.1-2/48B

Gentiles are idolaters, and Israelites worship the one, true God, who has made himself known in the Torah. In the Talmud that is the difference — the only consequential distinction — between Israel and the gentiles. But the Halakhah takes as its religious problem the concretization of that distinction, the demonstration of where and how the distinction in theory makes a huge difference in the practice, the conduct, of everyday affairs. What is at stake is that Israel stands for life, the gentiles like their idols for death. An asherah-tree, like a corpse, conveys uncleanness to those who pass underneath it, thus at M. Abodah Zarah 3:8: "And he should not pass underneath it, but if he passed underneath it, he is unclean." The Talmud explicitly classifies an idol as a corpse:

BAVLI ABODAH ZARAH 3:8A-C II.1-2/48B
A. [48B] One should not sit in [an *asherah's*] shade, but if he sat in its shade, he is clean.

B. And he should not pass underneath it, but if he passed underneath it, he is unclean.
C. If it was overshadowing public domain, taking away property from public use, and one passed beneath it, he is clean.

II.1 A. And he should not pass underneath it, but if he passed underneath it, he is unclean:
B. What is the operative consideration [that leads us to say he is unclean]?
C. It is simply not possible that there will be no remnants of offerings to idols under the tree.

II.2 A. Who is the authority behind this unassigned rule?
B. It is R. Judah b. Beterah, for it has been taught on Tannaite authority:
C. How on the basis of Scripture do we know that the remnant of an offering to an idol imparts uncleanness by means of overshadowing to all that are located within its shadow? As it is said, 'They joined themselves also to Baal Peor and ate the sacrifices of the dead' (Ps. 106:28): just as a corpse conveys uncleanness by means of overshadowing to all that are located within its shadow, so what has been offered to an idol conveys uncleanness by means of overshadowing to all that are located within its shadow.

The upshot is simple: idols and idolaters are like corpses. When idolaters die, they are condemned to the grave forever. Israel stands up from the grave and gains the world to come. To be an Israelite is to live, and to look forward to eternal life. Why, then, does idolatry define the boundary between Israel and everybody else? The reason is that idolatry — rebellious arrogance against God — encompasses the entire Torah. The religious duty to avoid idolatry is primary; if one violates the religious duties, he breaks the yoke of commandments, and if he violates that single religious duty, he violates the entire Torah. Violating the prohibition against idolatry is equivalent to transgressing all Ten Commandments.

The Halakhah treats gentiles as undifferentiated, but as individuals. The Aggadah treats gentiles as "the nations" and takes no interest in individuals or in transactions between private persons. In the theology of the Talmud, the category, the gentiles or the nations, without elaborate differentiation, encompasses all who are not-Israelites, that is, who do not belong to Israel and therefore do not know and serve God. That category takes on meaning only as complement and opposite to its generative counterpart, having no standing — self-defining characteristics — on its own. That is, since Israel encompasses the sector of humanity that knows and serves God by reason of God's self-manifestation in the Torah, the gentiles are comprised by everybody else: those placed by their own intention and active decision beyond the limits of God's revelation. Guided by the Torah Israel worships God, without its illumination gentiles worship idols. At the outset, therefore, the main point registers: by "gentiles" sages understand, God's enemies, and by "Israel" sages understand, those who know God as God has made himself known, which is, through the Torah. In no way do we deal with secular categories, but with theological ones.

The Halakhah then serves as the means for the translation of theological conviction into social policy. Gentiles are assumed to be ready to murder any Israelite they can get their hands on, rape any Israelite women, commit bestiality with any Israelite cow. The Talmud cites few cases to indicate that that conviction responds to ordinary, everyday events; the hostility to gentiles flows from a theory of idolatry, not the facts of everyday social intercourse, which, as we have seen, sages recognize is full of neighborly cordiality. Then why take for granted gentiles routinely commit the mortal sins of not merely idolatry but bestiality, fornication, and murder? That is because the Halakhah takes as its task the realization of the theological principle that those who hate Israel hate God, those who hate God hate Israel, and God will ultimately vanquish Israel's enemies as his own — just as God too was redeemed from Egypt. So the theory of idolatry, involving alienation from God, accounts for the wicked conduct imputed to idolaters, without regard to whether, in fact, that is how idolaters conduct themselves. Idolatry is what angers God and turns him against the gentiles, stated in so many words at b. A.Z. 1:1 I.23/4b: "That time at which God gets angry comes when the kings put on their crowns on their heads and prostrate themselves to the sun. Forthwith the Holy One, blessed be He, grows angry." That is why it is absolutely forbidden to conduct any sort of commerce with gentiles in connection with occasions of idolatrous worship, e.g., festivals and the like.

Why do sages define a principal category of the Halakhah in this wise? It is because sages must devote a considerable account to the challenge to that justice represented by gentile power and prosperity, Israel's subordination and penury. For if the story of the moral order tells about justice that encompasses all creation, the chapter of gentile rule vastly disrupts the account. Gentile rule forms the point of tension, the source of conflict, attracting attention and demanding explanation. For the critical problematic inherent in the category, Israel, is that its anti-category, the gentiles, dominates. So what rationality of a world ordered through justice accounts for the world ruled by gentiles represents the urgent question to which the system must respond. And that explains why the systemic problematic focuses upon the question, how can justice be thought to order the world if the gentiles rule? That formulation furthermore forms the public counterpart to the private perplexity: how is it that the wicked prosper and the righteous suffer? The two challenges to the conviction of the rule of moral rationality — gentile hegemony, matched by the prosperity of wicked persons — match.

Yet here the Halakhah turns out to make its own point, one that we ought not to miss. The Halakhah presupposes not gentile hegemony but only gentile power; and it further takes for granted that Israelites may make choices, may specifically refrain from trading in what gentiles value in the service of their gods, and may hold back from gentiles what gentiles require for that service. In this regard the

Halakhah parts company from the Aggadah, the picture gained by looking inward not corresponding to the outward-facing perspective. Focused upon interiorities that prove real and tangible, not matters of theological theory at all, the Halakhah of Abodah Zarah legislates for a world in which Israelites, while subordinate in some ways, control their own conduct and govern their own destiny. Israelites may live in a world governed by gentiles, but they form intentions and carry them out. They may decide what to sell and what not to sell, whom to hire for what particular act of labor and to whom not to sell their own labor, and, above all, Israelite traders may determine to give up opportunities denied them by the circumstance of gentile idolatry.

The Halakhah therefore makes a formidable statement of Israel's freedom to make choices, its opportunity within the context of everyday life to preserve a territory free of idolatrous contamination, must as Israel in entering the Land was to create a territory free of the worship of idols and their presence. In the setting of world order Israel may find itself subject to the will of others, but in the house of Israel, Israelites can and should establish a realm for God's rule and presence, free of idolatry. And if to establish a domain for God, Israelites must practice self-abnegation, refrain from actions of considerable weight and consequence, well, much of the Torah concerns itself with what people are not supposed to do, and God's rule comes to realization in acts of restraint.

Accordingly, the religious problem of the Halakhah therefore focuses on the inner world of Israel in command of itself. The religious problem of the Aggadah , by contrast, explains, rationalizes as best it can, gentile hegemony such as the Halakhah takes for granted gentiles simply do *not* exercise. For the Halakhah sees that world within Israel's dominion for which Israel bears responsibility; there sages legislate. The Aggadah forms a perspective upon the world subject to gentile rule, that is, the world beyond the limits of Israel's own power. The Halakhah speaks of Israel at the heart of matters, the Aggadah , of Israel within humanity.

Gentiles, by reason of their condition outside of the Torah, are characterized by certain traits natural to their situation, and these are worldly. Not only so, but the sages' theology of gentiles shapes the normative law in how to relate to them. If an Israelite is by nature forbearing and forgiving, the gentile by nature is ferocious. That explains why in the Halakhah as much as in the Aggadah gentiles are always suspect of the cardinal sins, bestiality, fornication, and bloodshed, as well as constant idolatry. That view of matters is embodied in normative law, as we have seen. The law of the Mishnah corresponds to the lore of scriptural exegesis; the theory of the gentiles governs in both. Beyond the Torah there not only is no salvation from death, there is not even the possibility of a common decency. The Torah makes all the difference. The upshot may be stated very simply. Israel and the gentiles form the two divisions of humanity. The one will die but rise from the grave to eternal life with God. When the other dies, it perishes; that is the end. Moses said it very well: Choose life. The gentiles sustain comparison and contrast with Israel, the point of ultimate division being death for the one, eternal life for the other.

If Israel and the gentiles are deemed comparable, the gentiles do not acknowledge or know God, therefore, while they are like Israelites in sharing a common humanity by reason of mythic genealogy — deriving from Noah — the gentiles do not receive in a meritorious manner the blessings that God bestows upon them. So much for the points of stress of the Aggadah. When it comes to the Halakhah, as we have seen, the religious problematics focuses not upon the gentiles but upon Israel: what, given the world as it is, can Israel do in the dominion subject to Israel's own will and intention? That is the question that the Halakhah fully answers. For the Halakhah constructs, indeed defines, the interiority of an Israel sustaining God's service in a world of idolatry: life against death in the concrete and tangible dimensions by which life is sustained: trade and the production of food (wine). No wonder Israel must refrain from engaging with idolatry on days of the festivals for idols that the great fairs embody — then especially.

4

The Talmud's Union of Halakhah and Aggadah

The Halakhah of Self-denial on the Day of Atonement and the Aggadah of Repentance

I. RITE AND RIGHT. THE FATHERS ACCORDING TO RABBI NATHAN IV:V.2

Critical to Rabbinic theology, atonement for sin is attained, in the Halakhah as in Scripture, through Temple rites of offerings. These involve a clear specific of the sin that is atoned for, so the correct attitude is essential. But the Aggadic complement to the Halakhic requirements made the right attitude — repentance — essential to the righting of the Israelite's relationship with God.

No transaction is so encumbered by ritual as Temple offerings, and none more subject to prophetic criticism, with its emphasis on God's quest for the human heart: "For I desire mercy and not sacrifice, and the knowledge of God rather than burnt offerings" (Hos. 6:6). Ethical and moral conduct contrasts with Temple sacrifices not only in prophetic writings, Amos for example, but also in the Rabbinic comment on how atonement is attained beyond the age of the Temple, with the altar in ruins and barren of Israel's offerings:

THE FATHERS ACCORDING TO RABBI NATHAN IV:V.2

A. One time [after the destruction of the Temple in August, 70] Rabban Yohanan ben Zakkai was going forth from Jerusalem, with R. Joshua following after him. He saw the house of the sanctuary lying in ruins.

B. R. Joshua said, "Woe is us for this place that lies in ruins, the place in which the sins of Israel used to be atoned for."

C. He said to him, "My son, do not be distressed. We have another mode of atonement, which is like [atonement through sacrifice], and what is that? It is deeds of loving kindness.

D. "For so it is said, 'For I desire mercy and not sacrifice, and the knowledge of God rather than burnt offerings' (Hos. 6:6)."

Atonement for sin, principal consideration of the offerings in the Temple, could be attained in another medium altogether: deeds not of rite but of right. And the Halakhah, with its stress on right action, depended on its Aggadic complement to make that point in the very context of a highly ritualistic transaction, that of the atonement-rites of the Day of Atonement.

That is because the ritualization, in Temple offerings, of relationships between Israel and God nowhere comes to more elaborate expression than in the observance of the Day of Atonement, which in Lev. 16:1-34 is described as a sequence of atonement-rites. The Halakhah of the Mishnah, as amplified in the Talmud, presents the offerings of the Day of Atonement as a narrative, following Scripture's program. Since Lev. 16:29 calls also for the practice of self-denial ("afflict your souls") in atonement for sin, the Halakhah set forth at tractate Yoma, devoted to the Day of Atonement, turns to the rules that pertain to fasting, refraining from work: "For on this day atonement shall be made for you to cleanse you of all your sins, you shall be clean before the Lord. It shall be a Sabbath of complete rest for you, and you shall practice self-denial" (JPS). The Aggadah of the pertinent chapter of the Talmud links atonement to repentance, completely recasting the topic at hand, and it is at that point that the union of the Halakhah and the Aggadah makes its theological statement.

The pertinent verses of Scripture are as follows, with the one pertinent item underlined:

> The Lord spoke to Moses after the death of the two sons of Aaron, when they drew near before the Lord and died, and the Lord said to Moses, "Tell Aaron your brother not to come at all times into the holy place within the veil, before the mercy seat which is upon the ark, lest he die; for I will appear in the cloud upon the mercy seat. But thus shall Aaron come into the holy place, with a young bull for a sin offering and a ram for a burnt offering. He shall put on the holy linen coat and shall have the linen breeches on his body, be girded with the linen girdle, and wear the linen turban; these are the holy garments. He shall bathe his body in water and then put them on. And he shall take from the congregation of the people of Israel two male goats for a sin offering and one ram for a burnt offering.
>
> "And Aaron shall offer the bull as a sin offering for himself and shall make atonement for himself and for his house. Then he shall take the two goats and set them before the Lord at the door of the tent of meeting; and Aaron shall cast lots upon the two goats, one lot for the Lord and the other lot for Azazel. And Aaron shall present the goat on which the lot fell for the Lord and offer it as a sin offering; but the goat on which the lot fell for Azazel shall be presented alive before the Lord

4. The Talmud's Union of Halakhah and Aggadah... 69

to make atonement over it, that it may be sent away into the wilderness to Azazel.

"Aaron shall present the bull as a sin offering for himself and shall make atonement for himself and for his house; he shall kill the bull as a sin offering for himself. And he shall take a censer full of coals of fire from the altar before the Lord, and two handfuls of sweet incense beaten small; and he shall bring it within the veil and put the incense on the fire before the Lord, that the cloud of the incense may cover the mercy seat which is upon the testimony, lest he die. And he shall take some of the blood of the bill and sprinkle it with his finger on the front of the mercy seat and before the mercy seat he shall sprinkle the blood with his finger seven times.

"Then he shall kill the goat of the sin offering which is for the people and bring its blood within the veil and do with its blood as he did with the blood of the bull, sprinkling it upon the mercy seat and before the mercy seat; thus he shall make atonement for the holy place, because of the uncleannesses of the people of Israel, and because of their transgressions, all their sins; and so he shall do for the tent of meeting, which abides with them in the midst of their uncleanness. There shall be no man in the tent of meeting when he enters to make atonement in the holy place until he comes out and has made atonement for himself and for his house and for all the assembly of Israel. Then he shall go out to the altar that is before the Lord and make atonement for it; and shall take some of the blood of the bull and of the blood of the goat and put it on the horns of the altar round about. And he shall sprinkle some of the blood upon it with his finger seven times and cleanse it and hallow it from the uncleanness of the people of Israel.

"And when he has made an end of atonement for the holy place and the tent of meeting and the altar, he shall present the live goat; and Aaron shall lay both his hands upon the head of the live goat; and confess over him all the iniquities of the people of Israel, all their transgressions and all their sins; and he shall put them upon the head of the goat and send him away into the wilderness by the hand of a man who is in readiness. The goat shall bear all their iniquities upon him to a solitary land; and he shall let the goat go in the wilderness.

"Then Aaron shall come into the tent of meeting and shall put off the linen garments which he put on when he went into the holy place and shall leave them there; and he shall bathe his body in water in a holy place and put on his garments and come forth and offer his burnt offering and the burnt offering of the people and make atonement for himself and for the people. And the fact of the sin offering he shall burn upon the altar. And he who lets the goat go to Azazel shall wash his clothes and bathe his body in water and afterward he may come into the camp. And the bull for the sin offering and the goat for the sin offering, whose blood was brought in to make atonement in the holy place, shall be carried forth outside the camp; their skin and their flesh and their dung shall be burned with fire. And he who burns them shall wash his clothes and bathe his body in water and afterward he may come into the camp.

"It shall be a statute for you for ever that in the seventh month, on the tenth day of the month, you shall afflict yourself and shall do no work, either the native or the stranger who sojourns among you; for on this day shall atonement be made for you, to cleanse you, from all your sins you shall be clean before the Lord. It is a Sabbath of solemn rest to you, and you shall afflict yourselves; it is a statute for ever. And the priest who is anointed and consecrated as priest in his father's place shall make atonement, wearing the holy linen garments; he shall make atonement for the sanctuary and he shall make atonement for the tent of meeting and for the altar and he shall make atonement for the priests and for all the people of the assembly. And this shall be an everlasting statute for you, that atonement may be made for the people of Israel once in the year because of their sins." And Moses did as the Lord commanded him.

Leviticus 16:1-34

What is blatant is the omission of all consideration of attitude; here atonement is a matter of action only. The presentation of the Halakhah, rather than its contents, forms the center of interest in the present case. The Aggadah contributes the introduction of a theme invited by, but not present in, the narrative itself, the theme of repentance. The Aggadah's contribution focuses upon the centrality of Israel's attitude — here, the power of the repentant spirit — in the very heart and center of the cult itself. The Halakhah of self-denial then encompasses the Aggadic exposition of the requirement of repentance as a pre-requisite of atonement, and in that union of Halakhah and Aggadah the Day of Atonement is transformed.

II. BAVLI YOMA CHAPTER EIGHT. AN OVERVIEW

The Halakhah that forms the point at which the Aggadah intervenes, Mishnah-tractate Yoma Chapter Eight, concerns not eating, drinking, and performing other everyday actions, all in the name of self-denial on the Day of Atonement. The Mishnah's statement of the law is amplified throughout. An abbreviated outline of the Mishnah and the principal propositions of the Gemara's compositions suffices to show the way in which the Halakhah on its own shapes the topic. Only with an overview before us will the radical shift contributed by the Aggadic exposition of an intersecting theme be fully appreciated in context.

This outline of the Gemara's exposition of the Mishnah covers an entire chapter of the Talmud. We see the intellectual program that governs and can follow the exposition of the entire theme of repentance, Halakhic and Aggadic components in context. The Mishnah's text is in lower case caps and bold face type; other principal propositions of the exposition are in lower case caps and regular type.

4. The Talmud's Union of Halakhah and Aggadah... 71

Then I give only the proposition of the complete compositions that follow, showing the relationship of the parts to the whole.

MISHNAH-TRACTATE YOMA 8:1-2

A. ON THE DAY OF ATONEMENT IT IS FORBIDDEN TO (1) EAT, (2) DRINK, (3) BATHE, (4) PUT ON ANY SORT OF OIL, (5) PUT ON A SANDAL, (6) OR ENGAGE IN SEXUAL RELATIONS.
  1. I:1: Is it merely forbidden? The man is subject to the penalty of extirpation!
     a. I:2: And is it the fact that in any passage in which the Tannaite formulation declares the penalty to be extirpation, the language of prohibition is not used at all as is the premise of the opening question?
  2. I:3: Reversion to a detail of I:1: As to half of the requisite volume of forbidden substance — R. Yohanan said, "It is forbidden by the law of the Torah." And R. Simeon b. Laqish said, "It is permitted by the law of the Torah."

B. COMPOSITE ON THE AFFLICTION OF SOULS ON THE DAY OF ATONEMENT, IN PARTICULAR, THROUGH FASTING
  1. I:4: Tannaite complement: "You shall afflict your souls" (Lev. 16:29) — might one suppose that a person should therefore sit in the sun or in the cold so as to suffer anguish? Just as the prohibition of work means, sit and do nothing, so the commandment to afflict one's soul means, sit and do nothing by abstinence.
  2. I:5: Tannaite complement as above, with the resolution: Just as the prohibition of work covers a matter for which in another context one would incur liability on the Sabbath in particular, so the affliction of the soul covers something for which in another context one would incur liability. And what might that be? This would refer to eating meat of a sacrifice that has been subjected by the officiating priest to an improper intention or eating meat that has been left over and not burned at the required time.
  3. I:6: "You shall afflict your souls" (Lev. 16:29) — here we find a reference to affliction, and elsewhere we find a reference to the same matter. Just as elsewhere, the affliction concerns hunger, so here the affliction must concern hunger.

C. APPENDIX ON THE AFFLICTION THAT INVOLVES EATING: THE CASE OF MANNA
  1. I:7: "Who fed you in the wilderness with manna...that he might afflict you" (Dt. 8:16) — R. Ammi and R. Assi — One said, "One who has a loaf of bread in his basket is not the same as one

who has no loaf of bread in his basket. And one said, "One who sees what he is eating is not the same as one who does not see while he is eating."

    a.   I:8: Continuation of Ammi & Assi composite; an interpolated proposition tangential in the foregoing.
    b.   I:9: Continuation of Ammi & Assi composite.
    c.   I:10: Continuation of Ammi & Assi composite.
        I.   I:11: Thematic add-on.

2. I:12: "We remember the fish that we used to eat in Egypt for nothing" (Num. 11:5) — Rab and Samuel: "Real fish" vs. "A euphemism for sexual relations."
3. I:13: "The cucumbers and the melons" (Ex. 11:5) — "In the manna they tasted every sort of food but not the taste of the five specified items, cucumbers, melons, leeks, onions, and garlic."
4. I:14: "Now the manna was like coriander seed" (Num. 11:7) — "It was round like coriander seed and white like pearl."
    a.   I:15: Tannaite complement: "Now the manna was like coriander seed" (Num. 11:7): — the letters for the word for coriander bears the meaning that the manna was like flax seed in its capsules.
    b.   I:16: Tannaite complement: The letters for the word for coriander bear the meaning that the manna told the Israelites whether an infant was born at nine months, after intercourse with the first husband, or at seven months, after intercourse with the second husband.
        I.   I:17: Just as the prophet told the Israelites what was to be found in clefts or holes, so manna would reveal to Israelites what was in the clefts and holes.
5. I:18: "And when the dew fell upon the camp in the night, the manna fell upon it" (Num. 11:9). "And the people shall go and gather" (Ex. 16:4). "The people went about and gathered it" (Num. 11:8) — how so?
6. I:19: It is written "bread" and also "dough of cakes" and "they ground it" (Num. 11:8) — how so?
7. I:20: "...or beat it in mortars" (Num. 11:8) — This teaches that with the man there descended for the Israelites women's cosmetics, that is, things that are ground in a mortar.
8. I:21: "And boiled it in pots" (Num. 11:8) — This teaches that with the manna there descended for the Israelites the makings of a pudding.
9. I:22: "And they brought yet to him freewill offerings every morning" (Ex. 36:3) — What is the meaning of every morning?

4. The Talmud's Union of Halakhah and Aggadah...

Precious stones and jewels descended from heaven and were given by the people as freewill offerings.

10. I:23: "And the taste of it was like the taste of a cake baked with oil" (Num. 11:8) — Just as the infant tastes at the breast any number of tastes, so for the manna, whenever the Israelites ate it, they found in it a whole variety of flavors.
11. I:24: "And Moses said, This shall be when the Lord shall give you in the evening meat to eat and in the morning bread to the full" (Ex. 16:8) — Meat, for which they asked not in the right way, was given to them at the wrong time. Bread, for which they asked in the right way, was given to them at the right time.
12. I:25: "While the meat was yet between their teeth" (Num. 11:33). And it is written, "But a whole month" (Num. 11:20) — how so? The middling folk died on the spot, the wicked suffered pain for a whole month.
13. I:26: "And they spread them all abroad" (Num. 11:32) — "Don't read, 'they spread abroad' but read the same letters with the vowels that yield, 'they were slaughtered.' This teaches that the Israelites incurred the penalty of being slaughtered."
14. I:27: "And they spread them all abroad" (Num. 11:32) —
15. I:28: It is written, "bread," and also "oil," and also "honey" (Ex. 16:29, 31, Num. 11:8). Which was it? Said R. Yosé b. R. Hanina, "For the young, bread; for the old, oil, for the children, honey."
16. I:29: The word for quail is written to be pronounced *shlaw* but we pronounce it as *slaw*. What does this mean? Said R. Hanina, "When the righteous eat it, it is at ease, but when the wicked eat it, it is like thorns for them."
    a. I:30: Said R. Hanan bar Raba, "There are four kinds of quail, and these are they: thrush, partridge, pheasant, and quail."
18. I:31: It is written, "And when the Said R. Yosé b. R. Hanina, "Drew on top, dew on the bottom; it looked like something put in a box."
19. I:32: "A fine scale-like thing" (Num. 11:9 — Said R. Simeon b. Laqish, "It is something that melts on the palm of the hand." R. Yohanan said, "It is something that is absorbed by the two hundred and forty-eight parts of the human body."
20. I:33: Tannaite complement: "Man did eat the bread of the mighty" (Ps. 78:25) — "It is the bread that the ministering angels eat," the words of R. Aqiba.
21. I:34: "But now our soul is dried away, there is nothing at all" (Num. 11:6) — They said, "This manna is going to dry up their bowels. For is there any born of woman who takes in but doesn't excrete?" the words of R. Aqiba.

22. I:35: His disciples asked R. Simeon b. Yohai, "How come the manna came down to the Israelites only once a year?"
23. I:36: Now R. Tarfon and R. Ishmael and sages were in session, dealing with the passage on manna, and R. Eleazar the Modite was in session among them. R. Eleazar the Modite responded and say, "The manna that came down for Israel was sixty cubits high."
    a. I:37: Issi b. Judah says, "The manna that came down for Israel kept ascending until all the kings of the east and west saw it, as it is said, 'You prepare a table before me in the presence of my enemies, my cup runs over' (Ps. 23:5, 6)."
24. I:38: Continuation of I:36.

D. ...TO (1) EAT, (2) DRINK:
    1. II:1: As to these five afflictions, to what do they correspond?
        a. II:2: Expansion on a secondary development of the foregoing.

E. ...(3) BATHE, (4) PUT ON ANY SORT OF OIL:
    1. III:1: How on the basis of Scripture do we know that refraining from bathing or putting on oil is classified as affliction?
        a. III:2: Secondary exegesis of the proof-text of III:1: What is the meaning of "I ate no pleasant bread"?
    2. III:3: How on the basis of Scripture do we know that refraining from putting on oil is classified as affliction?
    3. III:4: How on the basis of Scripture do we know that refraining from putting on oil is classified as affliction?
        a. III:5: Secondary expansion of the proof-text cited at III.1, 4.
    4. III:6: Another proof concerning how on the basis of Scripture do we know that refraining from putting on oil is classified as affliction?

F. ...(5) PUT ON A SANDAL,
    1. IV:1: How on the basis of Scripture do we know that refraining from wearing sandals is an affliction?

G. ...(6) OR ENGAGE IN SEXUAL RELATIONS:
    1. V:1: How on the basis of Scripture do we know that refraining from sexual relations is classified as affliction?

H. APPENDIX ON THE PROHIBITION AGAINST WASHING ON THE DAY OF ATONEMENT
    1. V:2: Tannaite complement: It is equally forbidden to wash part of one's body as the whole of one's body. But if one's hands were filthy with mud or shit, he may wash in the usual manner and not concern himself.

4. The Talmud's Union of Halakhah and Aggadah...

    2. V:3: Tannaite complement: A woman may rinse one hand in water to give bread to an infant and need not concern herself.
    3. V:4: Tannaite complement: If he was going to receive his father, master, or disciple, he crosses over the sea or river in the normal way, even up to his neck, and need not scruple.
        a. V:5: A set of illustrative cases.
    4. V:6: Continuation of V:4: As to walking through water up to one's neck objected R. Joseph, But even on a weekday is such an action permitted?
        a. V:7: And what is the rule concerning the Sabbath, on which people may wear sandals? May they walk through water wearing them?
    5. V:8: On the Day of Atonement it is forbidden to sit in mud.
    6. V:9: On the Day of Atonement it is permitted to cool off by sitting on fruit.
        a. V:10: Illustrative stories.

I. APPENDIX ON THE PROHIBITION OF WEARING SHOES ON THE DAY OF ATONEMENT
    1. V:11: A story yields the question, What is the law about wear on the Day of Atonement sandals of bamboo?
    2. V:12: Minors are permitted to do all of them except putting on sandals, for appearance's sake.

J. BUT A KING AND A BRIDE WASH THEIR FACES. "AND A WOMAN WHO HAS GIVEN BIRTH MAY PUT ON HER SANDAL'" THE WORDS OF R. ELIEZER. AND SAGES PROHIBIT.
    1. VI:1: Who is the authority behind this anonymous Mishnah-rule?

K. HE WHO EATS A LARGE DATE'S BULK OF FOOD, INCLUSIVE OF ITS PIT...:
    1. VII:1: As to the date's bulk of which they have spoken, does it include the pit or does it not include the pit?
    2. VII:2: The large date of which they have spoken is bigger than an egg's bulk, and it is an established fact for our rabbis that by that means one's hunger is sated, but with less than that volume one's hunger will not be sated.
    3. VII:3: The large date of which they have spoken is less in volume than an egg.
    4. VII:4: All standard measures for foods are the bulk of an olive, except for the minimum volume required for food to contract uncleanness, because in that case Scripture has used a different expression, on which account sages have imposed a distinct volume. Proof for the view derives from Scripture's presentation of the law of the Day of Atonement.

- a. VII:5: Amplification of a detail in the foregoing: How on the basis of Scripture do we know that the minimum volume required for food to contract uncleanness is an egg's bulk? Said R. Abbahu said R. Eleazar, "Said Scripture, 'All food therein that may be eaten' (Lev. 11:34) — this refers, then, to food that derives from that which also is edible, and what might that be? It is the egg of a hen."
   - i. VII:6: Continuation of foregoing: R. Eleazar, "He who eats forbidden fat at this time must record the volume, since another court may come along and impute to the requisite measures a larger volume."
- b. VII:7: Continuation of VII:5: The laws covering measurements of minimal quantities, and penalties constitute law revealed to Moses at Sinai.

L. OR HE WHO DRINKS THE EQUIVALENT IN LIQUIDS TO A MOUTHFUL IS LIABLE.
1. VIII:1: Not literally 'a mouthful,' but the volume is any case in which if he moved the liquid to one side of his mouth it would look like a mouthful would be a violation.

M. ALL SORTS OF FOODS JOIN TOGETHER TO FORM THE VOLUME OF THE DATE'S BULK, AND ALL SORTS OF LIQUIDS JOIN TOGETHER TO FORM THE VOLUME OF A MOUTHFUL.
1. IX:1: Said R. Pappa, "If one ate a piece of raw meat with salt, they join together to form the requisite volume to incur liability, and that is so even though salt is not really classified as a food, for, since people do eat it, it joins together."
2. IX:2: Said R. Simeon b. Laqish, "The brine on green vegetables joins with the vegetables to form the requisite volume to incur liability for a date's bulk on the Day of Atonement."
3. IX:3: Said R. Simeon b. Laqish, "He who eats too big a meal on the Day of Atonement is exempt from penalty. How come? '...who does not afflict...' (Lev. 23:29) is what Scripture has said, excluding the eating of a meal that brings discomfort."

N. HE WHO EATS AND HE WHO DRINKS — THESE PROHIBITED VOLUMES DO NOT JOIN TOGETHER TO IMPOSE LIABILITY FOR EATING OR FOR DRINKING, RESPECTIVELY.
1. X:1: Who is the Tannaite authority behind this statement?

MISHNAH-TRACTATE YOMA 8:3

A. IF ONE ATE AND DRANK IN A SINGLE ACT OF INADVERTENCE, HE IS LIABLE ONLY FOR A SINGLE SIN OFFERING. IF HE ATE AND DID A PROHIBITED ACT OF LABOR, HE IS LIABLE FOR TWO SIN OFFERINGS.

4. The Talmud's Union of Halakhah and Aggadah...

1. I:1: Explaining the absence of "you shall not" in connection with the prohibition of eating or drinking or acts of labor, said R. Simeon b. Laqish, "Now come no explicit admonition is mentioned in connection with the commandment to afflict oneself? It is because it is not possible to formulate one.
2. I:2: An effort to formulate a valid admonition such as Simeon b. Laqish says is not possible.
3. I:3: As above: A Tannaite authority of the household of R. Ishmael stated, "Here we find a reference to afflicting the soul, and elsewhere we find reference to afflicting the soul. Just as in the latter case, there is no penalty unless there has been a prior admonition, so here too there can be no penalty unless there is a prior admonition.
4. I:4: As above: We derive the fact by analogy between the phrase, 'a solemn day of rest' that occurs in connection with an everyday Sabbath and the same usage that occurs with reference to the Day of Atonement. Just as in the that case, there is no penalty unless there has been a prior admonition, so here too there can be no penalty unless there is a prior admonition. R. Pappa said, "The Day of Atonement itself is called the Sabbath, for said Scripture, 'In the ninth day of the month, from evening to evening, you shall keep your Sabbath' (Lev. 23:32)."

B. IF HE ATE FOODS WHICH ARE NOT SUITABLE FOR EATING, OR DRANK LIQUIDS WHICH ARE NOT 'SUITABLE FOR DRINKING —
  1. II:1: One who chews pepper on the Day of Atonement is exempt from punishment. If he chewed ginger on the Day of Atonement, he is exempt.
  2. II:2: Tannaite complement: one who eats leaves of calamus, he is liable, of vine, liable.

C. IF HE DRANK BRINE OR FISH BRINE — HE IS EXEMPT.
  1. III:1: Who is the Tannaite authority behind our Mishnah-rule, which holds one culpable for drinking vinegar?
     a. III:2: Secondary story.

MISHNAH-TRACTATE YOMA 8:4

A. AS TO CHILDREN, THEY DO NOT IMPOSE A FAST ON THEM ON THE DAY OF ATONEMENT. BUT THEY EDUCATE THEM A YEAR OR TWO IN ADVANCE, SO THAT THEY WILL BE USED TO DOING THE RELIGIOUS DUTIES.
  1. I:1: Since they educate the children two years in advance, can there be any question about doing so one year in advance? Of course we do so, and why should the Mishnah include that detail?
  2. I:2: In the case of girls, at the age of eight and nine, they educate them to fast for a few hours of the day, at the age of ten and

eleven, they finish out the day, by the authority of rabbis, and at twelve, they finish out the day by the authority of the Torah.

Mishnah-Tractate Yoma 8:5

A. A PREGNANT WOMAN WHO SMELLED FOOD AND GREW FAINT — THEY FEED HER UNTIL HER SPIRITS ARE RESTORED.

    1. I:1: Tannaite complement: A pregnant woman who smelled meat in the status of Holy Things or pig meat — for her they stick a reed into the juice and put it on her mouth. If she recovers, well and good, and if not, they feed her the gravy itself. If she recovers, well and good, but if not, they feed her the permitted fat itself, for there is nothing at all that stands ahead of the saving of life.

        a. I:2: Illustrative case: There was a pregnant woman who smelt something. They came before Rabbi. He said to her, "Go and whisper to her that today is the Day of Atonement."

B. A SICK PERSON — THEY FEED HIM ON THE INSTRUCTION OF EXPERTS. IF THERE ARE NO EXPERTS AVAILABLE, THEY FEED HIM ON HIS OWN INSTRUCTIONS, UNTIL HE SAYS, "ENOUGH."

    1. II:1: If the patient says he needs and the physician says he does not need food, they obey the patient.

    2. II:2: We have learned in the Mishnah: A sick person — they feed him on the instruction of experts. Are we then to conclude, on the instruction of experts yes, but on his own initiation no? On the instruction of a plurality of experts yes, but on the instruction of a single expert no?

    3. II:3: ...they feed him on the instruction of experts — *that's obvious!* We're dealing with a case of doubt concerning the saving of life, and a doubt concerning the saving of life is resolved in a lenient way.

    4. II:4: Mar bar R. Ashi said, "In any case in which the patient said, 'I need to eat,' even though there are a hundred who say he does not need to eat, we listen to him, since it is said, 'The heart knows its own bitterness' (Prov. 14:10)."

Mishnah-Tractate Yoma 8:6-7

A. HE WHO IS SEIZED BY RAVENOUS HUNGER — THEY FEED HIM, EVEN UNCLEAN THINGS, UNTIL HIS EYES ARE ENLIGHTENED.

    1. I:1: Tannaite complement: How do they know that his eyes are enlightened? Sufficient so that he knows the difference between good and bad food.

    2. I:2: Tannaite complement: He who was seized by blinding hunger — they feed him that which violates the law in least possible

measure. If there were before him untithed produce and carrion, they feed him carrion.
3. I:3: Tannaite complement: He who was seized by blinding hunger — they feed him honey and all kinds of sweets, for honey and sweets enlighten one's eyes.
4. I:4: He who was seized by blinding hunger — they feed him the fat tail with honey.
5. I:5: Said R. Yohanan, "Once I was seized by blinding hunger, so I ran to the east side of a fig tree..."
6. I:6: R. Judah and R. Yosé were going along the way, and R. Judah was seized by blinding hunger. He jumped a shepherd and ate his bread. Said to him R. Yosé, "You have jumped a shepherd." A second "going along the way" story is affixed here.

B. HE WHO WAS BITTEN BY A CRAZY DOG — THEY DO NOT FEED HIM A PIECE OF ITS LIVER'S LOBE. AND R. MATTIA B. HARASH PERMITS DOING SO.

C. APPENDIX ON THE TOPIC OF MAD DOGS
1. II:1: Tannaite complement: Five statements were made concerning a mad dog
2. II:2: What is the source of the madness in a dog?

D. FURTHER DID R. MATTIA B. HARASH SAY, "HE WHO HAS A PAIN IN HIS THROAT — THEY DROP MEDICINE INTO HIS MOUTH ON THE SABBATH:
1. III:1: R. Yohanan suffered from scurvy. He went to a certain matron. She made him something on Thursday and on Friday. He said to her, "So what should I do on the Sabbath?"
2. III:2: When R. Yohanan suffered from scurvy, he would put on this remedy on the Sabbath and was healed. This he did in accord with Mattia's ruling in the Mishnah.

E. BECAUSE IT IS A MATTER OF DOUBT AS TO DANGER TO LIFE. AND ANY MATTER OF DOUBT AS TO DANGER TO LIFE OVERRIDES THE PROHIBITIONS OF THE SABBATH."
1. IV:1: Why was it necessary to go on and say further, And any matter of doubt as to danger to life overrides the prohibitions of the Sabbath?
2. IV:2: Tannaite complement: They remove debris for one whose life is in doubt on the Sabbath. And the one who is prompt in the matter, lo, this one is to be praised. And it is not necessary to get permission from a court. How so? If one saw a child fall into the ocean and cannot climb up, or if his ship is sinking in the sea, and he cannot climb up, he spreads a net and pulls him out of there. And it is not necessary to get permission from a court.
3. IV:3: In matters having to do with danger to life, they are not guided by the condition of the majority.

F. HE UPON WHOM A BUILDING FELL DOWN — IT IS A MATTER OF DOUBT WHETHER OR NOT HE IS THERE, IT IS A MATTER OF DOUBT WHETHER IF HE IS THERE, HE IS ALIVE OR DEAD, IT IS A MATTER OF DOUBT WHETHER IF HE IS THERE AND ALIVE HE IS A GENTILE OR AN ISRAELITE — THEY CLEAR AWAY THE RUIN FROM ABOVE HIM.
   1. V:1: What's the point of this statement of hypothetical cases?
G. IF THEY FOUND HIM ALIVE, THEY REMOVE THE REMAINING RUINS FROM ABOVE HIM.
   1. VI:1: That's obvious!
H. BUT IF THEY FOUND HIM DEAD, THEY LEAVE HIM BE UNTIL AFTER THE SABBATH.
   1. VII:1: That too is obvious!
   2. VII:2: Tannaite complement: On the Sabbath, when people are removing debris, if the buried person gives no sign of life, how far is the debris removed? Until one reaches his nose.
   3. VII:3: How on the basis of Scripture do we know that danger to life overrides the restrictions of the Sabbath?

Now we reach the end of the Halakhic exposition and the intrusion of a theological proposition, fully expounded.

MISHNAH-TRACTATE YOMA 8:8-9
A. A SIN OFFERING AND AN UNCONDITIONAL GUILT OFFERING ATONE.
   1. I:1: A sin offering and an unconditional guilt offering atone: is it possible that while the guilt offering for a certain sin atones, a suspensive guilt offering does not? But lo, "atonement" is inscribed with reference to that too!
B. DEATH AND THE DAY OF ATONEMENT ATONE WHEN JOINED WITH REPENTANCE.
   1. II:1: That is the case only when joined with repentance, but not when not joined with repentance — then may we say that this does not accord with the position of Rabbi?
C. REPENTANCE ATONES FOR MINOR TRANSGRESSIONS OF POSITIVE AND NEGATIVE COMMANDMENTS.
   1. III:1: Since it is the fact that it atones for a negative commandment that has been violated, is there any need to specify that it also atones for a positive commandment that has been violated?
      a. III:2: Amplification of a detail of the foregoing.
D. COMPOSITE ON REPENTANCE
   2. III:3: The types of atonement that R. Ishmael expounded, with each of which repentance is required.
      a. III:4: Gloss of the foregoing. What is the definition of the profanation of the Divine Name?

4. The Talmud's Union of Halakhah and Aggadah...

    b.   III:5: Continuation of the topic of the foregoing.

1. III:6: Said R. Hama bar Hanina, "Great is repentance, which brings healing to the world: 'I will heal their backsliding, I will love them freely' (Hos. 14:5)."
2. III:7: Said R. Levi, "Great is repentance, which reaches up to the throne of glory: 'Return, Israel, to the Lord your God' (Hos. 14:2)."
3. III:8: Said R. Yohanan, "'Great is repentance, for it overrides a negative commandment that is in the Torah....'"
4. III:9: Said R. Jonathan, "Great is repentance, for it brings redemption near...."
5. III:10: Said R. Simeon b. Laqish, "Great is repentance, for by it sins that were done deliberately are transformed into those that were done inadvertently...."
6. III:11: Said R. Samuel bar Nahmani said R. Jonathan, "Great is repentance, for it lengthens the years of a person...."
7. III:12: Come and take note of how the characteristic of the Holy One, blessed be he, is not like the characteristic of mortals. If a mortal insults his fellow by something that he has said, the other may or may not be reconciled with him. And if you say that he is reconciled with him, he may or may not be reconciled by mere words. But with the Holy One, blessed be he, if someone commits a transgression in private, he will be reconciled with him in mere words.
8. III:13: R. Meir would say, "Great is repentance, for on account of a single individual who repents, the whole world is forgiven in its entirety."
9. III:14: How is a person who has repented to be recognized?
10. III:15: Said R. Judah, "Rab contrasted verses of Scripture: it is written, 'Happy is he whose transgression is covered, whose sin is pardoned' (Ps. 32:1), and further, 'He who covers his transgression shall not prosper' (Prov. 28:13). But there is no contradiction, the one speaks of a sin that is publicly known, the other of a sin that is not publicly known."
11. III:16: R. Yosé b. R. Judah says, "When a person does a transgression once, he is forgiven, a second time, he is forgiven, a third time, he is forgiven. But when he does it a fourth time, he is not forgiven: 'Thus says the Lord, for three transgressions of Israel, yes for four, I will not reverse it' (Amos 2:6); and further, 'Lo, all these things does God work, twice, yes, three times, with a man' (Job 33:29)."
12. III:17: Tannaite complement. Matters concerning which one has said confession on the preceding Day of Atonement, one does

not have to include in the confessions of the coming Day of Atonement, unless he did those same transgressions in the intervening year.

13. III:18: Tannaite complement. "And he has to specify each individual sin," the words of R. Judah b. Patera, as it is said, 'O Lord, these people have sinned a great sin land have made a god of gold' (Ex. 32:31)." R. Aqiba says, "It is not necessary to list each sin. If so, why does it say, 'And made a god of gold'? But: Thus did the Omnipresent say, 'Who made you make a god of gold? It is I, who gave you plenty of gold.'"

14. III:19: Two truly good providers arose for Israel, Moses and David. Moses said, "Let my sin be written down: 'because you believed not in me to sanctify me' (Num. 20:21)." David said, "Let mine not be written down: 'Happy is he whose transgression is forgiven, whose sin is pardoned' (Ps. 82:1)."

15. III:20: They make public hypocrites' evil deeds on account of the desecration of the divine name, as it is said, 'When a righteous man turns from his righteousness and commits iniquity and I lay a stumbling block before him, he shall die' (Ezek. 3:20) — to make public his hypocrisy.

16. III:21: Repentance of a confirmed sinner postpones punishment, and that is even though the decree against him of punishment has already been signed and sealed.

17. III:22: It is not good for the wicked to be shown respect in this world. It is good for the righteous not to be shown favor in this world.

18. III:23: He who brings merit to the community never causes sin: so that he will not end up in Gehenna, while his disciples are in the Garden of Eden. And he who causes the community to sin — they never give him a sufficient chance to attain penitence, so that he will not end up in the Garden of Eden, while his disciples are in the Gehenna: "

E. AND AS TO SERIOUS TRANSGRESSIONS, REPENTANCE SUSPENDS THE PUNISHMENT UNTIL THE DAY OF ATONEMENT COMES ALONG AND ATONES. HE WHO SAYS, "I SHALL SIN AND REPENT, SIN AND REPENT" — THEY GIVE HIM NO CHANCE TO DO REPENTANCE.

1. IV:1: Why repeat two times, sin and repent, sin and repent?

F. IF HE SAID, "I WILL SIN AND THE DAY OF ATONEMENT WILL ATONE," — THE DAY OF ATONEMENT DOES NOT ATONE.

1. V:1: May we say that our Mishnah-ruling is not in accord with Rabbi?

G. FOR TRANSGRESSIONS DONE BETWEEN MAN AND THE OMNIPRESENT, THE DAY OF ATONEMENT ATONES. FOR TRANSGRESSIONS BETWEEN MAN AND

4. The Talmud's Union of Halakhah and Aggadah... 83

MAN, THE DAY OF ATONEMENT ATONES, ONLY IF THE MAN WILL REGAIN THE GOOD WILL OF HIS FRIEND.
THIS EXEGESIS DID R. ELEAZAR B. AZARIAH STATE: "'FROM ALL YOUR SINS SHALL YOU BE CLEAN BEFORE THE LORD' (LEV. 16:30) — FOR TRANSGRESSIONS BETWEEN MAN AND THE OMNIPRESENT DOES THE DAY OF ATONEMENT ATONE. FOR TRANSGRESSIONS BETWEEN MAN AND HIS FELLOW, THE DAY OF ATONEMENT ATONES, ONLY IF THE MAN WILL REGAIN THE GOOD WILL OF HIS FRIEND." SAID R. AQIBA, "HAPPY ARE YOU, O ISRAEL. BEFORE WHOM ARE YOU MADE CLEAN, AND WHO MAKES YOU CLEAN? IT IS YOUR FATHER WHO IS IN HEAVEN, AS IT SAYS, 'AND I WILL SPRINKLE CLEAN WATER ON YOU, AND YOU WILL BE CLEAN' (EZ. 36:25). AND IT SAYS, O LORD, THE HOPE OF ISRAEL (JER. 17:13) — JUST AS THE IMMERSION POOL CLEANS THE UNCLEAN, SO THE HOLY ONE, BLESSED BE HE, CLEAN ISRAEL."

1. VI:1: R. Joseph bar Habu raised a contradiction to R. Abbahu, " For transgressions between man and man, the Day of Atonement atones, only if... — but it is written, 'If one man sin against his fellow man, God will pacify him' (1 Sam. 2:25)."
2. VI:2: Said R. Isaac, "Whoever offends his fellow, even if through what he says, has to reconcile with him."
    a. VI:3: Illustrative story: R. Abba had a complaint against R. Jeremiah, Jeremiah went and sat at the door of R. Abba. In the interval his serving girl through out slops. Some drops fell on his head. He said, "They've made a dung heap out of me," and about himself he cited the verse, "He raises up the poor out of the dust" (1 Sam. 2:8).
    b. VI:4: Illustrative story: When R. Zira had a quarrel with someone, he would pass by him repeatedly, so as to show himself to him, so that the other might come forth to seek reconciliation with him.
    c. VI:5: Illustrative story: Rab reconciled with someone he had offended.

H. COMPOSITE ON THE RECITATION OF THE CONFESSION

3. VI:6: Tannaite complement: The religious duty of saying the confession applies at the eve of the Day of Atonement at dusk. But sages have said, A man should say the confession before eating and drinking, lest he be distracted while eating and drinking.
4. VI:7: What does one say as the prayer of confession?
5. VI:8: On three occasions in the year priests raise up their hands in the priestly benediction four times a day, and these are they: (1) at the dawn prayer, (2) the additional prayer, (3) the afternoon prayer, and (4) the closing of the gates: on the occasion of fasts,

on the occasions of prayers of members of the delegation, and on the Day of Atonement (M. Ta. 4:1). What is the definition of the closing of the Temple gates?

    a. VI:9: Illustrative story. Ulla bar Rab went down to lead the congregation in prayer in the presence of Raba. He opened with, "You have chosen us...," and closed with, "What are we, what is our life." He praised him.

6. VI:10: The recitation of the Prayer at the closing of the gates exempts one from having to say the Evening Prayer.

    a. VI:11: Tannaite supplement to a subsidiary analysis of the foregoing.

With the entire program of the Talmud to Yoma Chapter Eight before us, we are in a position to see how the Aggadic component of the treatment of the rites of the Day of Atonement recasts the topic and reshapes the Halakhah in context.

III. THE HALAKHAH OF ATONEMENT AND THE AGGADAH OF REPENTANCE. BAVLI YOMA 8:9 III.3-VI.5/86A-87B

Clearly, the exposition of the theme of repentance is invited by the Halakhah, with its hierarchization of media of atonement, encompassing repentance. But repentance is not then situated within a ladder of such media; rather it is treated as an absolute requirement of atonement in any form, a considerable shift in the presentation of matters. Making repentance absolute, not relative to other conditions that produce atonement, imparts a judgment, as to proportion, that subverts the rite while affirming it.

Here is how in the very center of its Halakhic exposition, the Talmud situates its Aggadic response to the topic of self-denial on the Day of Atonement and what is required for atonement to take place on that day. We begin with a classification of types of atonement and the relationship of atonement and repentance.

COMPOSITE ON REPENTANCE
BAVLI YOMA 8:9 III.3-VI.5/86A-87B

III.3. A. In Rome R. Mattia b. Harash asked R. Eleazar b. Azariah, ""Have you heard about the four types of atonement that R. Ishmael expounded?"

    B. He said to him, "I heard indeed, but they are three, but with each of them repentance is required.

    C. "One verse of Scripture says, 'Return, you backsliding children, says the Lord, I will heal your backsliding' (Jer. 3:22). A second says,' For on this day shall atonement be made for you to cleanse you' (Lev. 16:30). And a third says, 'Then I will visit their transgression with the rod and their iniquity with strokes' (Ps.

89:33), and a fourth: 'Surely this iniquity shall not be expiated by you until you die' (Is. 22:14).

D. "How so? If someone has violated a religious duty involving an act of commission but has repented, he does not move from that spot before he is forgiven forthwith. In this regard it is said, 'Return, you backsliding children, says the Lord, I will heal your backsliding' (Jer. 3:22).

E. "If someone has transgressed a negative commandment but has repented, repentance suspends the punishment and the Day of Atonement atones. In this regard it is said, 'For on this day shall atonement be made for you to cleanse you' (Lev. 16:30).

E. "If someone has transgressed a rule, the penalty of which is extirpation or judicially inflicted capital punishment, but has repented, the repentance and the Day of Atonement suspend the matter, and suffering on the other days of the year effect atonement, and in this regard it is said, 'Then I will visit their transgression with the rod and their iniquity with strokes' (Ps. 89:33).

F. "But one who has profaned the name of heaven — repentance has not got the power to effect suspension of the punishment, nor suffering to wipe it out, nor the Day of Atonement to atone, but repentance and suffering suspend the punishment, and death will wipe out the sin with them, and in this regard it is said, 'Surely this iniquity shall not be expiated by you until you die' (Is. 22:14)" [Fathers According to R. Nathan XXIX:VIII.1] [cf. Tosefta Kippurim 4:10].

The work of glossing the foregoing composition gets under way with a series of definitions. The role of death in particular in atoning for sin is not amplified. In Chapter Seven we shall see how death and the atonement attained thereby open the way to the restoration of humanity to Eden, Israel to eternal life.

III.4. A. *What is the definition of the profanation of the Divine Name?*

B. *Said Rab, "For example, in my case, if I took meat from my butcher and didn't pay for it on the spot."*

C. *Said Abbayye, "That consideration pertains only where someone does not go collecting, but in a place where someone goes collecting what is owing, there is no objection to such conduct."*

D. *Said Rabina, "And Mata Mehasya is a place in which people go collecting."*

E. *When Abbayye would buy meat from two partners, he would give a zuz to this one and a zuz to that one, and then would bring them together and make a reckoning.*

F. *R. Yohanan said, "For example in, my case, if I were to walk four cubits without contemplation of Torah or wearing phylacteries."*

III.5. A. *R. Isaac of the household of R. Yannai said, "Anyone whose colleagues are ashamed by reason of his reputation — that is a profanation of the Divine Name."*

B. Said R. Nahman bar Isaac, "It is a case in which people say of someone, may his Master forgive Mr. So-and-So."
C. Abbayye said, "It is for example as has been taught on Tannaite authority: "'And you will live the Lord your God" (Dt. 6:4) — that the Name of Heaven may be made beloved through you, that one should recite Scripture and repeat Mishnah-teachings and serve as a disciple to disciples of sages, and so that one's give and take be done in serenity with other people. Then what will people say about him? "Happy is this one's father, who taught him Torah, happy is his master, who taught him Torah. Who for those people who have not studied Torah. Look at Mr. So-and-so, to whom they taught Torah — see how lovely are his ways, how orderly his deeds! Concerning him, Scripture says, "And he said to me, you are my servant, Israel, in whom I will be glorified" (Is. 49:3). But as to him who studies Scripture and repeats Mishnah and who serves as a disciple to disciples of sages but whose give and take is not in good faith and his speech is not serene with other people — what do people say about him? Who is Mr. So-and-So, who has studied Torah, woe is his father, who taught him Torah, woe is his master, who taught him Torah. As to Mr. So-and-so, who has studied Torah — see how disreputable are his deeds and how ugly his ways, and concerning him Scripture says, "In that men said of them, These are the people of the Lord and are gone forth out of his land" (Ez. 36:20).'"

Now the Talmud presents a series of free-standing topical expositions of the dominant theme, repentance.

III.6. A. Said R. Hama bar Hanina, "Great is repentance, which brings healing to the world: 'I will heal their backsliding, I will love them freely' (Hos. 14:5)."
B. *R. Hama bar Hanina contrasted verses:* "'Return you backsliding children' — *who to begin with were backsliding.* Vs. 'I will heal your backsliding' (Jer. 3:22). *There is no contradiction,* in the one case, the repentance is out of love, in the other, out of fear."
C. *R. Judah contrasted verses:* "'Return you backsliding children, I will heal your backsliding' (Jer. 3:22). Vs. 'For I am lord to you, and I will take you one of a city and two of a family' (Jer. 3:14). *There is no contradiction,* in the one case, the repentance is out of love or fear, in the other, repentance comes as a consequence of suffering."
III.7. A. Said R. Levi, "Great is repentance, which reaches up to the throne of glory: 'Return, Israel, to the Lord your God' (Hos. 14:2)."
III.8. A. [86B] Said R. Yohanan, "Great is repentance, for it overrides a negative commandment that is in the Torah: 'If a man put away his wife and she go from him and become another man's wife, may he

4. The Talmud's Union of Halakhah and Aggadah...

return to her again? Will not that land be greatly polluted? But you have played the harlot with many lovers, and would you then return to me, says the Lord' (Jer. 3:1)."

III.9. A. Said R. Jonathan, "Great is repentance, for it brings redemption near: 'And a redeemer shall come to Zion and to those who return from transgression in Jacob' (Is. 59:20) — how come 'a redeemer shall come to Zion'? Because of 'those who return from transgression in Jacob.'"

III.10. A. Said R. Simeon b. Laqish, "Great is repentance, for by it sins that were done deliberately are transformed into those that were done inadvertently: 'And when the wicked turns from his wickedness and does that which is lawful and right, he shall live thereby' (Ez. 33:19) — *now 'wickedness' is done deliberately, and yet the prophet calls it stumbling!*"

B. Is this so? But said R. Simeon b. Laqish, "Great is repentance, for by it sins that were done deliberately are transformed into those that were merits 'And when the wicked turns from his wickedness and does that which is lawful and right, he shall live thereby' (Ez. 33:19)"!

C. *There is no contradiction between these versions,* the one refers to repentance out of love, the other, out of fear.

III.11. A. Said R. Samuel bar Nahmani said R. Jonathan, "Great is repentance, for it lengthens the years of a person: 'And when the wicked turns from his wickedness...he shall live thereby' (Ez. 33:19)."

III.12. A. *Said R. Isaac, [or} they say in the West in the name of Rabbah bar Mari,* "Come and take note of how the characteristic of the Holy One, blessed be he, is not like the characteristic of mortals. If a mortal insults his fellow by something that he has said, the other may or may not be reconciled with him. And if you say that he is reconciled with him, he may or may not be reconciled by mere words. But with the Holy One, blessed be he, if someone commits a transgression in private, he will be reconciled with him in mere words, as it is said, 'Take with you words and return to the Lord' (Hos. 14:3). And not only so, but [God] credits it to him as goodness: 'and accept that which is good' (Hos. 14:5); and not only so, but Scripture credits it to him as if he had offered up bullocks: 'So will we render for bullocks the offerings of our lips' (Hos. 14:5). Not you might say that reference is made to obligatory bullocks, but Scripture says, 'I will heal their backsliding, I love them freely' (Hos. 14:5)."

III.13. A. *It has been taught on Tannaite authority:*

B. R. Meir would say, "Great is repentance, for on account of a single individual who repents, the whole world is forgiven in its entirety: 'I will heal their backsliding, I will love them freely, for my anger has turned away from him' (Hos. 14:5). What is said is not 'from them' but 'from him.'"

III.14. A. *How is a person who has repented to be recognized?*

B. Said R. Judah, "For example, if a transgression of the same sort comes to hand once, and second time, and the one does not repeat what he had done."

C. *R. Judah defined matters more closely:* "With the same woman, at the same season, in the same place."

III.15. A. *Said R. Judah, "Rab contrasted verses of Scripture:* it is written, 'Happy is he whose transgression is covered, whose sin is pardoned' (Ps. 32:1), and further, 'He who covers his transgression shall not prosper' (Prov. 28:13). *But there is no contradiction,* the one speaks of a sin that is publicly known, the other of a sin that is not publicly known."

B. R. Zutra bar Tobiah said R. Nahman [said], "The one speaks of transgressions between a person and his fellow, the other, transgressions between a person and the Omnipresent."

III.16. A. *It has been taught on Tannaite authority:*

B. R. Yosé b. R. Judah says, "When a person does a transgression once, he is forgiven, a second time, he is forgiven, a third time, he is forgiven. But when he does it a fourth time, he is not forgiven: 'Thus says the Lord, for three transgressions of Israel, yes for four, I will not reverse it' (Amos 2:6); and further, 'Lo, all these things does God work, twice, yes, three times, with a man' (Job 33:29)."

C. *What's the point of and further,?*

D. *Should you say, that is the case when the public is involved, but not in the case of an individual [the cited verse proves the contrary, which speaks of an individual, not all Israel].then come and take note:* "Lo, all these things does God work, twice, yes, three times, with a man" (Job 33:29).

What follows, III.17ff., are passages of the Tosefta that pertain, each one glossed and clarified.

III.17. A. *Our rabbis have taught on Tannaite authority:*

B. **Matters concerning which one has said confession on the preceding Day of Atonement, one does not have to include in the confessions of the coming Day of Atonement, unless he did those same transgressions [in the intervening year]. [If] he committed those transgressions, he must include them in the confession. [If] he did not commit those transgressions, but he included them in his confession — concerning such a person — the following is said: "As a dog returns to his vomit, so a fool returns to his folly" (Prov. 26:11). R. Eliezer b. Jacob says, "Lo, such a person is praiseworthy, since it is said, 'For I acknowledge my transgressions' (Ps. 51:3)"** [T. Kip. 4:15].

C. Then how do I deal with "As a dog returns to his vomit, so a fool returns to his folly" (Prov. 26:11)?

D. *It is in accord with R. Huna for* said R. Huna, "Once a person has committed a transgression and done it again, it is permitted to him."

4. The Talmud's Union of Halakhah and Aggadah...

      E.   "It is permitted to him" *do you say?*

      F.   *Rather, say,* It is transformed for him so that it appears to be permitted.

III.18. A.   "And he has to specify each individual sin," the words of R. Judah b. Baba, as it is said, 'O Lord, these people have sinned a great sin land have made a god of gold' (Ex. 32:31)."

      B.   R. Aqiba says, "It is not necessary [to list each sin], since it is said, 'Happy is he whose transgression is covered, whose sin is pardoned.' If so, why does it say, 'And made a god of gold'? But: Thus did the Omnipresent say, 'Who made you make a god of gold? It is I, who gave you plenty of gold'" [T. Kip. 4:14]. [Bavli's version: If so, why does it say, 'And made a god of gold'? It is in accord with R. Yannai, for said R. Yannai, 'Said Moses before the Holy One, blessed be he, The silver and gold that you showered on Israel until they said, "enough" is what has made them make golden idols.'"

III.19. A.   Two truly good providers arose for Israel, Moses and David. Moses said, "Let my sin be written down: 'because you believed not in me to sanctify me' (Num. 20:21)." David said, "Let mine not be written down: 'Happy is he whose transgression is forgiven, whose sin is pardoned' (Ps. 82:1)."

      B.   To what may Moses and David be compared? To the case of two women who were flogged by the court, one who had committed an indiscretion, the other who had eaten unripe figs of the seventh year [which should have been allowed to ripen]. So to them the one who had eaten unripe figs in the seventh year, "By your grace, announce on what account I am being flogged, so people will not say, 'For the same sin for which that one is being flogged, this one is being flogged.'" So they brought unripe figs of the seventh year and hung them around her neck and announced before her, saying, "It is because of matters having to do with the seventh year that she is being flogged."

III.20. A.   **They make public hypocrites' [evil deeds] on account of the desecration of the divine name, as it is said, 'When a righteous man turns from his righteousness and commits iniquity and I lay a stumbling block before him, he shall die' (Ezek. 3:20) — to make public his [hypocrisy] [T. Kip. 4:12E-F].**

III.21. A.   Repentance of a confirmed sinner postpones punishment, and that is even though the decree against him of punishment has already been signed and sealed.

      B.   The prosperity of the wicked ends in disaster.

      C.   Authority buries authorities.

      D.   Naked does one come in, naked does one go forth, and would that one's exodus be like his entry.

The practice of Rabbinic sages is now recorded, to exemplify right attitude and action. But the gloss has no bearing on repentance in particular, rather, an attitude of humility and fear of sin in general.

> E. *When Rab would come to court, he would say this, "With a bitter soul he goes forth to death. The needs of his house he has not attended to. He goes home empty-handed. Would that his coming home should be as is his going forth, and would that one's exodus be like his entry.*
> F. *When Raba went to court, he would say,* **[87A]** *"By his own volition he goes to death. The needs of his house he has not attended to. He goes home empty-handed. Would that his coming home should be as is his going forth, and would that one's exodus be like his entry. And when he saw the crowd escorting him, he would say, 'Though his excellence mount up to the heavens and his head reach unto the clouds, yet shall he perish forever, like his own dung' (Prov. 27:24)."*
> G. *When on the Sabbath that coincided with a festival people would lift up Mar Zutra the Pious onto their shoulders, he would say this, "'For riches are not for ever nor does the crown endure for all generations' (Prov. 27:24)."*

III.22. A. "It is not good to respect the person of the wicked" (Ps. 18:5) — It is not good for the wicked to be shown respect in this world.
B. It was not good for Ahab that he was shown favor in this world: "Because he humbled himself before me, I will not bring evil in his days" (1 Kgs. 21:29).
C. It is good for the righteous not to be shown favor in this world.
D. It was good for Moses not to be shown favor in this world: "Because you did not believe in me, to sanctify me" (Dt. 20:13). Lo, had you believed in me, the time for you to take leave of this world would not yet have come.
E. Happy are the righteous, for it is not sufficient for them only to acquire uncoerced grace in their own behalf but they bestow unmerited grace to their children and their grandchildren to the end of all generations.
F. For how many sins did Aaron have who were worthy of being burned up like Nadab and Abihu, as it is said, "That were left..." (Lev. 10:12), but the uncoerced grace attained by their father stood up for them.
G. Woe are the wicked, for it is not sufficient for them only to suffer condemnation on their own account, but they bring about the condemnation of their children and their grandchildren to the end of all generations.
H. Canaan had many sons who were worthy of being ordained like Tabi, Rabban Gamaliel's son, but the guilt of their ancestor caused them to lose out.

The exposition concludes with the limits of repentance: when no amount of repentance suffices. Involved is causing the entire community to sin.

III.23. A. He who brings merit to the community never causes sin. And he who causes the community to sin — they never give him a sufficient chance to attain penitence [M. Abot 5:18]:

B. He who brings merit to the community never causes sin: how come? It is so that he will not end up in Gehenna, while his disciples are in the Garden of Eden: "For you will not abandon my soul to the nether world nor will you suffer your godly one to see the pit" (Ps. 16:9).

C. And he who causes the community to sin — they never give him a sufficient chance to attain penitence: It is so that he will not end up in the Garden of Eden, while his disciples are in the Gehenna: "A man that is laden with the blood of any person shall hasten his steps to the pit, none will help him" (Prov. 28:17).

We now revert to the Mishnah's statements and take up the glossing of the concluding units. Here the Gemara conducts a rigorous clarification of the Aggadah as it routinely does of the Halakhah, the same sort of questions we have already met many times, e.g., why repeat language, is raised.

IV.1 A. [And as to serious transgressions, repentance suspends the punishment until the Day of Atonement comes along and atones.] He who says, "I shall sin and repent, sin and repent" — they give him no chance to do repentance.

B. *Why repeat two times,* sin and repent, sin and repent?

C. *It is in accord with what R. Huna said Rab said, for* said R. Huna said Rab, "Once a person has committed a transgression and done it again, it is permitted to him."

E. "It is permitted to him" *do you say?*

F. *Rather, say,* It is transformed for him so that it appears to be permitted.

V.1 A. If he said, "I will sin and the Day of Atonement will atone," — the Day of Atonement does not atone.

B. *May we say that our Mishnah-ruling is not in accord with Rabbi, for it has been taught on Tannaite authority:*

C. Rabbi says, "For all of the transgressions that are listed in the Torah, whether one has repented or not repented, the Day of Atonement attains atonement, except for one who breaks the yoke [of the kingdom of heaven from himself, meaning, denies God] and one who treats the Torah impudently, and the one who violates the physical mark of the covenant. In these cases if one has repented, the Day of Atonement attains atonement, and if not, the Day of Atonement does not attain atonement."

D. *You may even say that the rule accords with Rabbi's position. The situation in which he relies on [the Day of Atonement to attain atonement for sinning] is exceptional.*

VI.1 A. **For transgressions done between man and the Omnipresent, the Day of Atonement atones. For transgressions between man and man, the Day of Atonement atones, only if the man will regain the good will of his friend:**

B. *R. Joseph bar Habu raised a contradiction to R. Abbahu, " For transgressions between man and man, the Day of Atonement atones, only if... — but it is written, 'If one man sin against his fellow man, God will pacify him' (1 Sam. 2:25)."*

C. [He said to him,] "'God' here means, 'the Judge.'"

D. *Then note the continuation of the verse:* "But if a man sin against the Lord, who shall entreat for him"

E. *This is the sense of the statement:* "If a man sins against his fellow man the judge will judge him, and his fellow will forgive him, but if a man sins against the Lord God, who will entreat for him? Only repentance and good deeds."

The clause, "only if he will regain the good will of his friend" is now amplified, as the Mishnah-amplification gathers force.

VI.2.A. **[For transgressions between man and man, the Day of Atonement atones, only if the man will regain the good will of his friend:]** Said R. Isaac, "Whoever offends his fellow, even if through what he says, has to reconcile with him, as it is said, 'My son, if you have become surety for your neighbor, if you have struck your hands for a stranger, you are snared by the words of your mouth...do this now, my son, and deliver yourself, seeing you have come into the power of your neighbor, go, humble yourself, and urge your neighbor' (Prov. 6:1-3). If it is a money-claim against you, open the palm of your hand to him [and pay him off], and if not, send a lot of intermediaries to him."

B. Said R. Hisda, "He has to reconcile with him through three sets of three people each: 'He comes before men and says, I have sinned and perverted that which was right and it did not profit me' (Job 33:27)."

C. Said R. Yosé bar Hanina, "Whoever seeks reconciliation with his neighbor has to do so only three times: 'Forgive I pray you now...and now we pray you' (Gen. 50:17).

D. "And if he has died, he brings ten people and sets them up at his grave and says, 'I have sinned against the Lord the God of Israel and against this one, whom I have hurt."

VI.3.A. *R. Abba had a complaint against R. Jeremiah, [Jeremiah] went and sat at the door of R. Abba. In the interval his serving girl through out slops. Some drops fell on his head. He said, "They've*

4. The Talmud's Union of Halakhah and Aggadah...

made a dung heap out of me," *and about himself he cited the verse,* "He raises up the poor out of the dust" (1 Sam. 2:8).

B. *R. Abba heard and came out to him, saying, "Now I must come out to seek reconciliation with you: 'Go, humble yourself and urge your neighbor' (Prov. 6:1).*

VI.4. A. *When R. Zira had a quarrel with someone, he would pass by him repeatedly, so as to show himself to him, so that the other might come forth to seek reconciliation with him.*

B. *Rab had a fight with a certain butcher. The butcher did not come to him on the eve of the Day of Atonement, so he said, "I shall go and seek reconciliation with him."*

C. *R. Huna met him. He said to him, "Where is the master going?"*

D. *He said to him, "To seek reconciliation with Mr. So-and-so."*

E. *He thought, 'Abba [Rab] is going to bring about the other's death."*

F. *[Rab] went and stood by the man. The other was sitting and chopping up a beast's head. He raised his eyes and saw him. He said to him, "You're Abba, go away, I have no business to do with you." While he was chopping the head, a bone flew off, struck his throat, and killed him.*

VI.5. A. *Rab was expounding sections of Scripture for the rabbis, and R. Hiyya entered. [87B] So he started again. Then Bar Qappara came in, so he started again. Then R. Simeon b. Rabbi came in, so he started again. Then R. Hanina bar Hama came in. He said, "So much am I supposed to backtrack" So he did not go over it again.*

B. *R. Hanina was offended. Rab went to him on thirteen occasions of the eve of the Day of Atonement, but the other was not reconciled to him.*

C. *But how could he have behaved in such a way? And didn't R. Yosé bar Hanina say, "Whoever seeks pardon from his fellow should not seek it from him more than three times?"*

D. *Rab was exceptional.*

E. *And how could R. Hanina have behaved in such a way? And didn't Raba say, "Whoever is forbearing when he has a righteous claim — they bear with all of his sins."*

F. *Rather, R. Hanina saw in a dream that Rab was suspended on a palm tree, and there is a tradition that whoever is suspended from a palm tree becomes head. He said, "That implies that authority is going to be given to him," and he was not reconciled with him so that he would have to go and teach Torah in Babylonia.*

The thematic composite accomplishes the goal of linking atonement to repentance. This is the point at which the exposition of the Halakhah parts company from Scripture's account of matters in Leviticus 16. And it is the Aggadah that signals the new dimension that the Gemara wishes to impart to the theme. To understand what our compilers have accomplished, we have to call to mind the fundamental program of the Mishnah-tractate. All chapters but the final one are devoted to an exposition of the Temple rite on the Day of Atonement. Only the last chapter of the Mishnah-tractate, which we have examined in detail, systematically addresses the situation of the individual Israelite, not in the Temple cult, and how he observes the occasion.

The Mishnah-tractate through Chapter Seven, and consequently, the Gemara as well, therefore closely follows the presentation of the Day of Atonement at Leviticus Chapter Sixteen, which carefully catalogues the activities of the high priest on the holy day, but in a sentence or two suffices to tell ordinary folk how they are to conduct themselves. The challenge facing the Talmud-tractate framers, therefore, is to place the facts of the Mishnah's first seven chapters into a framework that accords proportion and balance to the claims of right in the very center of rite. That is to say, along with the exposition of the facts of Leviticus Chapter Sixteen as the Mishnah lays them out and complements them, the meaning of the Day of Atonement in the holy life of Israel the people has to be set forth. That is the achievement of the Aggadic complement before us.

IV. PROPHETIC THEOLOGY IN THE CONTEXT OF THE LAW: THE PRIORITY OF THE RIGHT ATTITUDE

It is only when we reach the concluding statements of the Halakhah that we move beyond the Halakhic reprise of the Torah's narrative. And then the presentation of the Halakhah tells us what is at stake, which is the prophetic reading of the cult. Sages understood the prophets' critique not as repudiation of the cult but as refinement of it, and in the very context of their account of the blood-rite they therefore invoke the prophets' norms alongside the Torah's. Jeremiah's call to repentance, Isaiah's reflections on the role of death in the penitential process, God's infinite mercy, Ezekiel's insistence on purity of spirit — these flow into the exposition of the Halakhah. Above all, sages underscore God's explicit promise to purify Israel, the promise set forth in Ezekiel's and Jeremiah's prophecies, cited at the end of the Mishnah-chapter:

> "From all your sins shall you be clean before the Lord' (Lev. 16:30) — for transgressions between man and the Omnipresent does the Day of Atonement atone. For transgressions between man and his fellow, the Day of Atonement atones, only if the man will regain the good will of his friend."

So the Halakhah, made explicit by the Aggadic topical appendix, recasts the entire category of the Day of Atonement, taking the theme of atonement to require an account of repentance, on the one side, and God's power to forgive and purify from sin, on the other. The main point is, the rites of atonement do not work *ex opere operato* but only conditionally. And it is the attitude and intention of the Israelite that set and meet that condition.

Two fundamental messages then register. First, the rites atone and so does death — but only when joined with repentance, and repentance reaches its climax in the cleansing effect of the occasion, the Day of Atonement itself: A sin-offering and an unconditional guilt-offering atone. Death and the Day of Atonement atone when joined with repentance. Repentance atones for minor transgressions of positive and negative commandments. And as to serious transgressions, [repentance] suspends the punishment until the Day of Atonement comes along and atones. But the entire system realizes its promise of reconciliation with God only on one condition: the Israelite to begin with must frame the right attitude. And that is one of sincerity and integrity: He who says, "I shall sin and repent, sin and repent" — they give him no chance to do repentance. "I will sin and the Day of Atonement will atone," — the Day of Atonement does not atone.

These statements, we realize, involve attitude and intentionality. They pertain not to the Day of Atonement nor even to the rites of penitence, but to the spirit in which the person acts when he has committed a sin and wishes to atone and repent. If in the commission of the sin he declares his conviction that his attitude makes no difference — I shall do what I want, and then repent in impunity — that attitude invoking pre-emptive atonement nullifies the possibility of repentance and the Day of Atonement to do their part in the work of reconciliation. And the Halakhah carries the matter still further, when it insists that, in the end, the attitude of the repentant sinner does not complete the transaction; the sinner depends also upon the attitude of the sinned-against. I cannot think of a more eloquent way of saying that the entire condition of Israel depends upon the inner integrity of Israel: the intentionality that motivates its actions, whether with God or with man.

The Aggadah represented here by the composite on repentance introduces into the representation of the theme of the Day of Atonement conceptions and considerations of which the Halakhic exposition of the Day of Atonement scarcely takes proportionate cognizance. Even the bulk of Chapter Eight, which we examined in detail for both the Mishnah and the Gemara, centers attention on right action in self-denial. It is only through the Aggadic complement to the Halakhah that the message registers: the Day of Atonement, which the Torah lays out as principally a Temple occasion, overspreads the world. That is not a merely-moral statement but one of cultic consequence, since we see the rite itself as one affecting the world beyond the Temple walls in the way in which the one analogous in its careful concern for the high priest's purification, the burning of the red cow, does. Israel's sin in the world intrudes into the cult, because the Temple, the mark of divine favor, was lost on account of Israel's sin, comparable to Adam's and Eve's loss of Eden.

But in line with the colloquy of Yohanan ben Zakkai and Joshua, his disciple, Israel's virtue intervenes. Israel's attitude and consequent action in everyday life registers, atones as offerings atone. That is because Israel's ordinary life compares with the Temple's sanctification; even as the Temple space is sanctified, so Israel's space is marked off by signs of the holy. Just as the Temple's priests display their riches in the ample cult, so Israel's sages display their resources of virtue and intellect in the service of the mind and heart, study of the Torah. And, it must follow, the righteousness represented by a life fearful of sin and rich in repentance, which comes to its climax on the Day of Atonement, infuses the entire people of Israel, not only the priesthood in the Temple on that same holy day.

The upshot is, the Mishnah's presentation of the Halakhah of the Day of Atonement, its recapitulation of the themes of Leviticus Chapter Sixteen in the proportions of Scripture's treatment of that topic, is both replicated and revised. The revision reaches it's climax in the Gemara's topical exposition of the Aggadah of repentance, as we saw. But the framers of the Halakhah in the Mishnah have invited the introduction of such a revision of the context in which the Halakhah takes its place. For it is the Halakhic authorities of the Mishnah in Mishnah-tractate Yoma Chapter Eight who at the end introduced the theme of repentance into the rite of atonement and insisted upon the centrality of the human will in the process of reconciliation. So in their daring and imaginative recasting of the dimensions of Yoma, the framers of the Gemara in amplifying the pertinent statements of the Mishnah have grasped and simply amplified the generative principle of the Halakhah of the Mishnah: atonement depends upon the world beyond the sanctuary and what happens there. But how far have the Halakhic theologians strayed from the message that God himself revealed to the prophets cited in the Mishnah, Isaiah, Jeremiah, Ezekiel, and the rest? All they have done is see things whole and in proportion.

Accordingly, what for Leviticus 16 and the first seven chapters of Mishnah-tractate Yoma forms a cultic occasion, in which Israel participates as bystanders, emerges in the Halakhic and Aggadic presentations of the Mishnah and the Tosefta and Bavli-tractate Yoma as an event in the life of holy Israel, in which all Israel bears tasks of the weight and consequence that, on that holy day, the High Priest uniquely carries out. On the Day of Atonement, holy Israel joins the high priest in the Holy of Holies; this they do every day by acts of loving kindness, and on that day by repentance and by afflicting themselves through fasting and other forms of abstinence, as the Written Torah requires. The Day of Atonement, the occasion on which the high priest conducts the rite in the privacy of the Holy of Holies, emerges transformed: the rites are private, but the event is public; the liturgy is conducted in the holy Temple, but the event bears its consequences beyond its walls, where sins are atoned for in the setting of the everyday and the here and now. What is singular and distinct — the rites of atonement on the holiest day of the year in the holiest place in the world — now makes its statement about what takes place on every day of the year in the ordinary life of everyday Israel. That is the logic — joining rite to right — of the Halakhah encompassing the Aggadah, the Torah of Leviticus 16 read in light of Isaiah, Jeremiah, and Ezekiel.

And that is how the Day of Atonement would make its way through time, not the sacrificial rite of the high priest in the Temple, but the atonement-celebration of all Israel in the world. What mattered to the compilers of Leviticus and the

Mishnah alike was the timeless performance of atonement through the bloody rites of the Temple What captured the attention of the framers of the Bavli-tractate, by contrast, was the personal discipline of atonement through repentance on the Day of Atonement and a life of virtue and Torah-learning on the rest of the days of the year. They took out of the Holy of Holies and brought into the homes and streets of the holy people that very mysterious rite of atonement that the Day of Atonement called forth. And they translated it into humanity's terms and context. In presenting the topic beyond the limits of the Halakhah, through the Aggadah they transformed the presentation the day and its meaning, transcending its cultic limits. And it was their vision, and not the vision of Leviticus Sixteen and the Mishnah's tractate, that would prove definitive.

From antiquity to our own day, the Day of Atonement would enjoy the loyalty of the people of Israel come what may, gaining the standing of Judaism's single most widely observed occasion. That fact attests to the power of the distinctive ideas set forth by the Halakhah and the Aggadah in tandem to transform a sacerdotal narrative into a medium of the inner, moral sanctification for Israel. On the occasion of the Day of Atonement the holy people wherever they are enter into the status of the holy priest and the locus of the Temple's inner sanctum and bring about the transaction between humanity and God that awaited since Eden: God and humanity reconciled through humanity's own regeneration: attitude realized in action, Aggadah in Halakhah.

5

The Talmud's Union of Halakhah and Aggadah

The Halakhah of Criminal Justice and the Aggadah of the Resurrection of the Dead

I. CRIMINAL JUSTICE, DEATH AND RESURRECTION. MISHNAH-TRACTATE SANHEDRIN 6:2, 5. BAVLI SANHEDRIN 4:5 VI.1/39B

The profound, chronic question facing monotheism, with its one, all-powerful, just and merciful God, concerns why the righteous suffer while the wicked prosper. In its acute form, the question faces every generation of monotheists: how come God allows such manifest injustice as the world manifests every day? The logic of monotheism takes over. If this life and this world tell the entire tale of humanity's fate, then monotheism collapses on the contradiction between promise and performance. The doctrine of the resurrection of the dead at the end of days, the last judgment, and (nearly) all Israel's entry into the world to come or the restored Eden resolves matters.

The story of a life does not end at the grave. All are judged, and those who are justified enter into eternal life. Those who do not "stand in judgment" at the end of time perish. So justice ultimately is done.¹ Without reward and punishment, judgment and perdition for the wicked, eternal life for the righteous, this world's imbalance cannot be righted, nor can God's justice be revealed. Monotheism without an eschatology — a theory of last things and of the end time — of judgment and the world to come leaves unresolved the tensions inherent in the starting point: God is one, God is just and merciful.

That doctrine of last things, critical to the full working of monotheist theology, promises eternity for those that stand in judgment at the end, and denies the world to come for those that do not. The prosperity of the wicked in this world masks their comeuppance in the last judgment, and the suffering of the righteous in this age underscores their reward in the world to come. They righteous atone for sin in the here and now and enter upon Eden. This life, therefore, forms the vestibule for the life to come, and the tale of divine justice continues beyond death.

How to express this theological doctrine of theodicy, the justification of God's works, through eschatology, the theory of last things? The Halakhah of the Mishnah, amplified by the Gemara, treats issues of death and resurrection in the context of its systematic account of criminal justice, its administration and program. Tractate Sanhedrin sets forth a full account of the institutions and procedures of civil and criminal justice, the imposition of the death penalty for specified actions, and the promise of resurrection, or the denial of resurrection, to certain classes of sinners or criminals. There is no missing the theological point of the legal exposition, the Aggadic soul of the Halakhic body.

The Talmud viewed whole thus expounds issues of repentance and atonement in the setting of the death penalty. This it does by encompassing resurrection for the final judgment and entry into the world to come in the context of penalties for sins and crimes (there is no difference for this system). Most of those subject to the death penalty complete atonement for sin or crime by suffering that penalty and join all Israel in the final judgment. A few exceptions to the rule underscore the ultimate promise of life eternal for all Israel, meaning, those who know and serve God.

The Mishnah systematically portrays the facts of the matter, and the Gemara links those facts to Scripture, and clarifies, harmonizes, and systematizes them. The Aggadah, outlined in what follows and sampled only in part, reinforces that message in three ways. First, it insists on a systematic demonstration that the resurrection of the dead for judgment and life eternal forms an integral teaching of the Torah of Sinai. Second, it explores the relationship between the creation and fall of humanity, at the beginning of human history, and the redemption and restoration of humanity to Eden, at the end of human history. So it finds in the model of beginnings the design for the end-time. Third, it frames a theory — several competing theories, really — of the place of the Messiah in the narrative of the end of days.

In Chapter Five we have already seen how the Halakhah provides for atonement of sin. But that covers only part of the story. For the sinner atones through not only self-denial, repentance, the Day of Atonement, suffering, and the like, but also through death, which effects atonement for all sins of all sinners, with few specified exceptions. On the other side of the grave, at the resurrection of the dead, Israelites are called to judgment and, sinless by reason of atonement realized through death, all Israelites but a few are welcomed into the world or age to come. All the unresolved issues of monotheism — the inequities of this world, the suffering of the righteous and prosperity of the wicked, the conflict of justice and mercy —

come to a logical resolution in the doctrine of resurrection and judgment. Then all things are made right at the end, and God's original plan for humanity, eternal life of bliss in God's own presence, is realized.

But how to express the Aggadah of the resurrection of the dead within the Halakhic system fully exposed by the Talmud? The union of the Aggadic doctrine of the resurrection of the dead with the Halakhah set forth in the criminal justice system, takes place in Sanhedrin's Gemara. That exposition of the Mishnah by the Gemara, as we shall see, defines the context in which resurrection is fully spelled out. How the law of punishment for crime or sin serves as the medium for so profoundly theological a doctrine is simple. Among the criminal penalties are not only corporal and capital punishment, but denial of the world to come to a small number of individuals and a small set of classes of persons as well. For them, death does not suffice to atone for the unique sins they have committed. They suffer ultimate extinction.

That is what defines the stakes in this critical component of sages' account of God's abode in Israel. What the Halakhah wishes to explore is, how is the Israelite sinner or criminal rehabilitated, through the criminal justice system, so as to rejoin Israel in Eden for eternity. The answer is, the criminal or sinner remains Israelite, no matter what he does — even though he sins — and the death-penalty exacted by the earthly court So the Halakhah of Sanhedrin embodies these Aggadic principles: [1] Israel endures for ever, encompassing (nearly) all Israelites; [2] sinners or criminals are able to retain their position within that eternal Israel by reason of the penalties that expiate the specific sins or crimes spelled out by the Halakhah; [3] it is an act of merciful justice that is done when the sinner or criminal is put to death, for at that point, he is assured of eternity along with everyone else. God's justice comes to full expression in the penalty, which is instrumental and contingent; God's mercy endures forever in the forgiveness that follows expiation of guilt through the imposition of the death penalty in this world, preparing the way to life eternal for the sinner or criminal.

That theological doctrine of the Aggadah accounts for the detailed Halakhic exposition of the correct form of the capital penalty for each capital sin or crime. The punishment must fit the crime within the context of the Torah in particular so that, at the resurrection and the judgment, the crime will have been correctly expiated. Because the Halakhah rests on the premise that God is just and that God has made man in his image, after his likeness, the Halakhah cannot deem sufficient that the punishment fit the crime. Rather, given its premises, the Halakhah must pursue the issue, what of the sinner once he has been punished? And the entire construction of the continuous exposition of Sanhedrin aims at making this simple statement: the criminal, in God's image, after God's likeness, pays the penalty for his crime in this world but like the rest of Israel will stand in justice and, rehabilitated, will enjoy the world to come.

So the religious principle that comes to expression in the Talmud of Sanhedrin concerns the meaning of man's being made in God's image. That means, it is in man's nature to surpass the grave. And how, God's being just, does the sinner or criminal survive his sin or crime? It is by paying with his life in the here and now, so that at the resurrection, he may regain life, along with all Israel. That is why the climactic moment in the Halakhah comes at the end of the long catalogue of those sins and crimes penalized with capital punishment. It is with ample reason that the Bavli places at the conclusion and climax of its version the ringing declaration, "all Israel has a portion in the world to come, except...." And the exceptions pointedly do not include any of those listed in the long catalogues of persons executed for sins or crimes.

That the two religious principles just now specified play a critical role in the formulation and presentation of the Halakhah of Sanhedrin is made explicit in the context of legal exposition itself. The rite of stoning involves an admonition that explicitly declares the death penalty the means of atoning for all crimes and sins, leaving the criminal blameless and welcome into the kingdom of Heaven:

MISHNAH-TRACTATE SANHEDRIN 6:2

A. [When] he was ten cubits from the place of stoning, they say to him, "Confess," for it is usual for those about to be put to death to confess.
B. For whoever confesses has a share in the world to come.
C. For so we find concerning Achan, to whom Joshua said, "My son, I pray you, give glory to the Lord, the God of Israel, and confess to him, [and tell me now what you have done; hide it not from me.] And Achan answered Joshua and said, Truly have I sinned against the Lord, the God of Israel, and thus and thus I have done" (Josh. 7:19). And how do we know that his confession achieved atonement for him? For it is said, "And Joshua said, Why have you troubled us? The Lord will trouble you this day" (Josh. 7:25) — This day you will be troubled, but you will not be troubled in the world to come.
D. And if he does not know how to confess, they say to him, "Say as follows: 'Let my death be atonement for all of my transgressions.'"

Within the very center of the Halakhic exposition comes the theological principle that the death-penalty opens the way for life eternal. It follows that at stake in tractate Sanhedrin is a systematic demonstration of how God mercifully imposes justice upon sinners and criminals, and also of where the limits to God's mercy are reached: rejection of the Torah, the constitution of a collectivity — an "Israel" — that stands against God. God's merciful justice then pertains to private persons. But there can be only one Israel, and that Israel is made up of all those who look forward to a portion in the world to come: who will stand in justice and transcend death. In humanity, idolators will not stand in judgment, and entire generations who sinned collectively as well as Israelites who broke off from the body of Israel and formed their own Israel do not enjoy that merciful justice that reaches full expression in the fate of Achan: he stole from God but shared the world to come. And so will all of those who have done the dreadful deeds catalogued in the Mishnah's part of the Talmud.

The religious principle expressed here — God's perfect, merciful justice, correlated with the conviction of the eternity of holy Israel — cannot have come to systematic statement in any other area of the Halakhah. That is because it is only in the present context that sages can have linked God's perfect, merciful justice to the concrete life of ordinary Israel, and it is only here that they can have invoked the certainty of eternal life to explain the workings of merciful justice. But there is more. Sages recognize that, in the setting of this life, the death penalty brings anguish, even though it assures the sinner or criminal expiation for what he has done. That matter is stated in so many words:

Mishnah-tractate Sanhedrin 6:5

A. Said R. Meir, "When a person is distressed, what words does the Presence of God say? As it were: 'My head is in pain, my arm is in pain'.

B. "If thus is the Omnipresent distressed on account of the blood of the wicked when it is shed, how much the more so on account of the blood of the righteous!"

God is distressed even at the blood of the wicked, even when it is shed in expiation for sin or crime. So while sages recognize the mercy and justice that are embodied in the sanctions they impose, they impute to God, and express in their own behalf, common sentiments and attitudes. They feel the same sentiments God does, as the exposition of the court process in tractate Sanhedrin Chapters Three and Four, cited presently, makes explicit.

That fact alerts us to the fundamental principle embodied in the Halakhah: man is responsible for what he does, because man is like God. That is the basis for penalizing sins or crimes, but it also is the basis for the hope for eternal life for nearly all Israel. Like God, man is in command of, and responsible for, his own will and intentionality and consequent conduct. The very fact that God reveals himself through the Torah, which man is able to understand, there to be portrayed in terms and categories that man grasps, shows how the characteristics of God and man prove comparable. The first difference between man and God is that man sins, but the one and the just God, never; connecting "God" and "sin" yields an unintelligible result. And the second difference between creature and Creator, man and God, is that God is God. That difference comes to the surface in a searing story cited in the epilogue, Chapter Eight.

It is not an accident that in the setting of the category-formation of Sanhedrin, sages set forth how God's emotions correspond with man's. Like a parent faced with a recalcitrant child, he takes no pleasure in man's fall but mourns. Not only so, but even while he protects those who love him, Israel, from his, and their, enemies, he takes to heart that he made all man; he does not rejoice at the Sea when Israel is saved, because, even then, his enemies are perishing. This is said in so many words in the context of a discussion on whether God rejoices when the wicked perish:

> BAVLI SANHEDRIN 4:5 VI.1/39B
>
> A. Therefore man was created alone [4:5J]:
> B. "And there went out a song throughout the host" (1 Kgs. 22:36) [at Ahab's death at Ramoth in Gilead].
> C. Said R. Aha b. Hanina, "'When the wicked perish, there is song' (Prov. 11:10).
> D. "When Ahab, b. Omri, perished, there was song."

Does God sing and rejoice when the wicked perish? Not at all:

> E. But does the Holy One, blessed be he, rejoice at the downfall of the wicked?
> F. Is it not written, "That they should praise as they went out before the army and say, 'Give thanks to the Lord, for his mercy endures forever' (2 Chr. 20:21),
> G. and said R. Jonathan, "On what account are the words in this psalm of praise omitted, 'Because he is good'? Because the Holy One, blessed be he, does not rejoice at the downfall of the wicked."

Now we revert to the conduct of God at the very moment of Israel's liberation, when Israel sings the Song at the Sea:

> H. For R. Samuel bar Nahman said R. Jonathan said, "What is the meaning of the verse of Scripture [that speaks of Egypt and Israel at the sea], 'And one did not come near the other all night' (Ex. 14:20)?
> I. "At that time, the ministering angels want to recite a song [of rejoicing] [the angels' daily song] before the Holy One, blessed be he.
> J. "Said to them the Holy One, blessed be he, 'The works of my hands are perishing in the sea, and do you want to sing a song before me?'"

Now the matter is resolved:

> K. Said R. Yosé bar Hanina, "He does not rejoice, but others do rejoice. Note that it is written, '[And it shall come to pass, as the Lord rejoiced over you to do good, so the Lord] will cause rejoicing over you by destroying you' (Deut. 28:63) — and not 'so will the Lord [himself] rejoice'"

L. That proves the case.

God's emotions correspond, then, to those of a father or a mother, mourning at the downfall of their children, even though their children have rebelled against them. Even at the moment at which Israel first meets God, with God's act of liberation at the Sea, God cannot join them in their song. God and Israel then correspond, the eternal God in heaven, Israel on earth, also destined for eternal life. Israel forms on earth a society that corresponds to the retinue and court of God in heaven. The Halakhah in its way, in Sanhedrin, says no less. Sanhedrin, devoted to the exposition of crime and just punishment, turns out to form an encompassing exercise in showing God's mercy, even, or especially, for the sinner or criminal who expiates the sin or crime: that concludes the transaction, but a great deal will follow it — and from it. In the context of the Torah I cannot think of any other way of making that statement stick than through the Halakhah of Sanhedrin: this sin, this punishment — and no more.

II. TRACTATE SANHEDRIN: AN OVERVIEW OF THE HALAKHAH

The Halakhah set forth in the Mishnah-tractate and systematically expounded in the Gemara of Sanhedrin deals with the organization of the Israelite government and courts and punishments administered thereby. The court system is set forth in the Mishnah's statement of matters at Mishnah-tractate Sanhedrin 1:1-5:5, the death-penalty at 6:1-9:4, and 11:6, and extra-judicial penalties at 9:5-6, 10:1-6. (The penalties other than capital are set forth in adjoining Talmud-tractate Makkot, covering perjury (with variable penalties), banishment, and flogging.) I present only the main points of the Mishnah's law. We meet the Gemara to Talmud Chapter Eleven in sections iii and iv, below.

I. THE COURT SYSTEM

A. VARIOUS KINDS OF COURTS AND THEIR JURISDICTION

M. 1:1 (1) Property cases [are decided] by three [judges]; (2) those concerning theft and damages, before three; (3) [cases involving] compensation for full-damages, half-damages [Ex. 21:35], twofold restitution [Ex. 22:3], fourfold and fivefold restitution [Ex. 21:37], by three; (4) cases involving him who rapes [Deut. 32:28-29], him who seduces [Ex. 22:15-16].
M. 1:4 (1) Cases involving the death penalty are judged before twenty-three judges. (2) The beast who commits or is subjected to an act of sexual relations with a human being is judged by twenty-three, since it is said, "And you will kill the woman and the beast" (Lev. 20:16).

and it says, "And the beast you will slay" (Lev. 20:15). (3) An ox which is to be stoned is judged by twenty-three, since it is said, "And the ox will be stoned, and also its master will be put to death" (Ex. 21:29). Just as [the case of the master], leading to the death-penalty, [is adjudged], so is the [case of] the ox, [leading to] the death-penalty. The wolf, lion, bear, panther, leopard, and snake a capital case affecting them is judged by twenty-three.

M. 1:5 (1) They judge a tribe, a false prophet [Deut. 18:20], and a high priest, only on the instructions of a court of seventy-one members. (2) They bring forth [the army] to wage a war fought by choice only on the instructions of a court of seventy-one. (3) They make additions to the city [of Jerusalem] and to the courtyards [of the Temple] only on the instructions of a court of seventy-one. (4) They set up sanhedrins for the tribes only on the instructions of a court of seventy-one. (5) They declare a city to be "an apostate City" [Deut. 13:12ff.] only on the instructions of a court of seventy-one.

B. THE HEADS OF THE ISRAELITE NATION AND THE COURT SYSTEM

M. 2:1 A high priest judges, and [others] judge him; gives testimony, and [others] give testimony about him; performs the rite of removing the shoe [Deut. 25:7-9], and [others] perform the rite of removing the shoe with his wife. [Others] enter levirate marriage with his wife, but he does not enter into levirate marriage, because he is prohibited to marry a widow.

M. 2:2 The king does not judge, and [others] do not judge him; does not give testimony, and [others] do not give testimony about him; does not perform the rite of removing the shoe, and others do not perform the rite of removing the shoe with his wife; does not enter into levirate marriage, nor [do his brother] enter levirate marriage with his wife. [Others] do not marry his widow.

C. THE PROCEDURES OF THE COURT SYSTEM: PROPERTY CASES

M. 3:1 Property-cases are [decided by] three [judges] [M. 1:1A]. This litigant chooses one [judge], and that litigant chooses one judge. The two judges choose one more..

M. 3:3 And these are those who are invalid [to serve as witnesses or judges]: he who plays dice; he who loans money on interest; those who race pigeons; and those who do business in the produce of the Seventh Year.

D. THE PROCEDURES OF THE COURT-SYSTEM: CAPITAL CASES

M. 4:1 The same [laws] apply to property cases and capital cases with respect to examination and interrogation [of witnesses], as it is said, "You will have one law" (Lev. 24:22).

M. 4:5 How do they admonish witnesses in capital cases? They would bring them in and admonish them [as follows]: "Perhaps it is your intention to give testimony on the basis of supposition, hearsay, or of what one witness has told another; [or you may be thinking], 'We heard it from a reliable person'" Or, you may not know that in the end we are going to interrogate you with appropriate tests of interrogation and examination. You should know that the laws governing a trial for property cases are different from the laws governing a trial for capital cases. In the case of a trial for property-cases, a person pays money and achieves atonement for himself. In capital cases [the accused's] blood and the blood of all those who were destined to be born from him [who was wrongfully convicted] are held against him [who testifies falsely] to the end of time."

M. 5:5 If they found him innocent, they sent him away. If not, they postpone judging him till the next day. They would go off in pairs and would not eat very much or drink wine that entire day, and they would discuss the matter all that night. And the next day they would get up and come to court. The one who favors acquittal says, "I declared him innocent [yesterday], and I stand my ground and declare him innocent today." And the one who declares him guilty says, "I declared him guilty [yesterday] and I stand my ground and declare him guilty today." The one who argues in favor of guilt may [now] argue in favor of acquittal, but the one who argues in favor of innocence may not now go and argue in favor of guilt. [If] they made an error in some matter, the two judges' clerks remind them [of what had been said].

II. THE DEATH PENALTY

A. STONING

M. 6:1 [When] the trial is over, [and the felon is convicted], they take him out to stone him. The place of stoning was well outside the court, as it is said, "Bring forth him who cursed [to a place outside the camp]" (Lev. 24:14). One person stands at the door of the courthouse, with flags in his hand, and a horseman is some distance from him, so that he is able to see him. [If] one [of the judges] said, "I have something to say in favor of acquittal," the one [at the door] waves the flags, and the horseman races off and stops [the execution]. And even if [the convicted party] says, "I have something to say in favor of my own acquittal," they bring him back, even four or five times, so long as there is substance in what he has to say. [If] they then found him innocent, they dismiss him, And if not, he goes out to be stoned. And a herald goes before him, crying out, "Mr. So-and-so, son of Mr. So-and-so, is going out to be stoned because he committed such-and-such a transgression, and Mr. So-and-so and Mr. So-and-so are the witnesses against him. Now anyone who knows grounds for acquittal — let him come and speak in his behalf!"

M. 6:2 [When] he was ten cubits from the place of stoning, they say to him, "Confess," for it is usual for those about to be put to death to confess. For whoever confesses has a share in the world to come. And if he does not know how to confess, they say to him, "Say as follows: 'Let my death be atonement for all of my transgressions.'"

M. 6:4 The place of stoning was twice the height of a man. One of the witnesses would push him over from the hips, so [hard] that he turned upward [in his fall]. He turned him over on his hips again [to see whether he had died]. [If] he had died thereby, that sufficed. If not, the second [witness] would take a stone and put it on his heart. [If] he died thereby, it sufficed. And if not, stoning him is [the duty] of all Israelites, as it is said, "The hand of the witnesses shall be first upon him to put him to death, and afterward the hand of all the people" (Deut. 17:7). Only the blasphemer and the one who worships an idol are hung. How do they hang him? They drive a post into the ground, and a beam juts out from it, and they tie together his two hands, and thus do they hang him. And they untie him forthwith. And if he is left overnight, one transgresses a negative commandment on his account, as it is said, "His body shall not remain all night on the tree, but you will surely bury him on the same day, for he who is hanged is a curse against God" (Deut. 21:23). that is to say, On what account has this one been hung? Because he cursed the Name, so the Name of Heaven turned out to be profaned.

M. 6:6 When the flesh had rotted, they [they do] collect the bones and bury them in their appropriate place,

B. <u>THE FOUR MODES OF EXECUTION THAT LIE IN THE POWER OF THE COURT AND HOW THEY ARE ADMINISTERED</u>

M. 7:1 Four modes of execution were assigned to the court, [listed in order of severity]: (1) stoning, (2) burning, (3) decapitation, and (4) strangulation.

C. STONING

M. 7:4 These are [the felons] who are put to death by stoning: He who has sexual relations with his mother, with the wife of his father, with his daughter-in-law, with a male, and with a cow; and the women who brings an ox on top of herself; and he who blasphemes, he who performs an act of worship for an idol, he who gives of his seed to Moloch, he who is a familiar spirit, and he who is a soothsayer; he who profanes the Sabbath, he who curses his father or his mother. he who has sexual relations with a betrothed maiden, he who beguiles [entices a whole town to idolatry], a sorcerer, and a stubborn and incorrigible son. He who has sexual relations with his mother is liable on her account because of her being his mother and because of her being his father's wife [Lev. 18:6-7, 20:11].

D. BURNING OR DECAPITATION

M. 9:1A-C And these are those who are put to death through burning: he who has sexual relations with both a woman and her daughter [Lev. 18:17, 20:14], and a priest's daughter who committed adultery [Lev. 21:9]. In the same category as a woman and her daughter are [the following]: his daughter, his daughter's daughter, his son's daughter, his wife's daughter, the daughter of her daughter, the daughter of her son, his mother-in-law, the mother of his mother-in-law, and the mother of his father-in-law.
M. 9:1Dff. And these are those who are put to death through decapitation: the murderer, and the townsfolk of an apostate town. A murderer who hit his neighbor with a stone or a piece of iron [Ex. 21:18], or who pushed him under water or into fire, and [the other party] cannot get out of there and so perished, he is liable.

E. STRANGULATION

M. 10:1 These are the ones who are to be strangled: he who hits his father and his mother [Ex. 21:15]; he who steals an Israelite [Ex. 21:16, Deut. 24:7]; an elder who defies the decision of a court, a false prophet, a prophet who prophesies in the name of an idol; He who has sexual relations with a married woman, those who bear false witness against a priest's daughter and against one who has sexual relations with her. He who hits his father and his mother is liable only if he will make a lasting bruise on them.

F. EXTRA-JUDICIAL PUNISHMENT

M. 9:5 He who was flogged [and did the same deed] and was flogged again — [if he did it yet a third time] the court puts him in prison and feeds him barley until his belly explodes. He who kills a someone not before witnesses they put him in prison and feed him the bread of adversity and the water of affliction (Is. 30:20).
M. 9:6 He who stole a sacred vessel [of the cult (Num. 4:7)], and he who curses using the name of an idol, and he who has sexual relations with an Aramaean woman — zealots beat him up [on the spot (Num. 25:8, 11)]. A priest who performed the rite in a state of uncleanness — his brothers, the priests, do not bring him to court. But the young priests take him outside the courtyard and break his head with clubs. A non-priest who served in the Temple — he is put to death] at the hands of Heaven.

G. DEATH FOR ALL ETERNITY: DENIAL OF ETERNAL LIFE

M. 11:1^2 All Israelites have a share in the world to come, And these are the ones who have no portion in the world to come: He who says, the resurrection of the dead is a teaching which does not derive from the Torah, and the Torah does not come from Heaven; and an Epicurean. [Section iii, following, sets forth the text of this chapter of the Mishnah and outlines the Gemara as well.]

What captures sages' interest in the topic is a hierarchization of sins or crimes as indicated by the severity of the penalties that are imposed, matched, also, by the formality and procedural punctiliousness of the courts' process. We move from property cases to capital cases, and, within capital cases, through the penalties for catalogued crimes from the heaviest to the lightest in context. Then, at the end, we turn to the most severe penalty of all — one that the earthly court cannot inflict but only the Heavenly court can impose. The auxiliary tractate that follows then proceeds from capital to corporal punishment.

So the order of the whole is [1] the earthly court and property cases; [2] the earthly court and capital punishment; [3] the heavenly court; and, appended in tractate Makkot, not abstracted here, [4] corporal punishment. The intent of the composition seen whole proves blatant. Promising an account of the courts and their procedures in adjudicating both property and capital cases, the Halakhah in

5. The Talmud's Union of Halakhah and Aggadah...

detail delivers a systematic exercise to show how the various sins or crimes defined by Scripture are hierarchized, leading to the climax — the worst possible penalty — of denial of a portion in the world to come, which is to say, life eternal beyond the grave.

III. BAVLI SANHEDRIN. AN OVERVIEW OF THE AGGADAH. THE EXPOSITION OF THE STATEMENT, "ALL ISRAEL HAS A PORTION IN THE WORLD TO COME"

The Gemara of Bavli-tractate Sanhedrin Chapter Eleven forms a dense and complex exposition of topics on last things, the end of days, the resurrection of the dead, and the like. An overview of the Gemara on M. 11:1-2, which forms a massive composite of topical expositions, affords perspective on how the Gemara has taken the statement of the Mishnah and vastly enriched it in a systematic way.

BAVLI SANHEDRIN 11:1-2

A. ALL ISRAELITES HAVE A SHARE IN THE WORLD TO COME, AS IT IS SAID, "YOUR PEOPLE ALSO SHALL BE ALL RIGHTEOUS, THEY SHALL INHERIT THE LAND FOREVER; THE BRANCH OF MY PLANTING, THE WORK OF MY HANDS, THAT I MAY BE GLORIFIED" (Is. 60:21).
AND THESE ARE THE ONES WHO HAVE NO PORTION IN THE WORLD TO COME: HE WHO SAYS, THE RESURRECTION OF THE DEAD IS A TEACHING WHICH DOES NOT DERIVE FROM THE TORAH:

1. I:1: On Tannaite authority it was stated, "Such a one denied the resurrection of the dead, therefore he will not have a portion in the resurrection of the dead. For all the measures meted out by the Holy One, blessed be he, are in accord with the principle of measure for measure."
2. I:2: How, on the basis of the Torah do we know about the resurrection of the dead? As it is said, "And you shall give thereof the Lord's heave-offering to Aaron the priest" (Num. 18:28). And will Aaron live forever? And is it not the case that he did not even get to enter the Land of Israel, from the produce of which heave-offering is given? Rather, this teaches that he is destined once more to live, and the Israelites will give him heave-offering. On the basis of this verse, therefore, we see that the resurrection of the dead is a teaching of the Torah.
   a. I:3: A Tannaite authority of the house of R. Ishmael taught, "'... to Aaron ...', 'like Aaron. That is to say, just as Aaron was in the status of an associate who ate his produce in a state of cultic cleanness even when not in the Temple, so his sons must be in the status of associates."
3. I:4: It has been taught on Tannaite authority: R. Simai says, "How

on the basis of the Torah do we know about the resurrection of the dead?"

4. I:5: Minim asked Rabban Gamaliel, "How do we know that the Holy One, blessed be he, will resurrect the dead?"

5. I:6: Romans asked R. Joshua b. Hananiah, "How do we know that the Holy One will bring the dead to life and also that he knows what is going to happen in the future?"

6. I:7: It has also been stated on Amoraic authority: Said R. Yohanan in the name of R. Simeon b. Yohai, "How do we know that the Holy One, blessed be he, will bring the dead to life and knows what is going to happen in the future?"

7. I:8: It has been taught on Tannaite authority: Said R. Eliezer b. R. Yosé, "In this matter I proved false the books of the minim. For they would say, 'The principle of the resurrection of the dead does not derive from the Torah.'"

   a. I:9: This accords with the following Tannaite dispute: "'That soul shall be utterly cut off' — 'shall be cut off' — in this world, 'utterly' — in the world to come," the words of R. Aqiba. Said R. Ishmael to him, "And has it not been said, 'He reproaches the Lord, and that soul shall be cut off' (Num. 15:31). Does this mean that there are three worlds? Rather: '... it will be cut off ...,' in this world, '... utterly ...,' in the world to come, and 'utterly cut off ...,' indicates that the Torah speaks in ordinary human language."

8. I:10: Queen Cleopatra asked R. Meir, saying, "I know that the dead will live, for it is written, 'And the righteous shall blossom forth out of your city like the grass of the earth' (Ps. 72:16). But when they rise, will they rise naked or in their clothing?"

9. I:11: Caesar said to Rabban Gamaliel, "You maintain that the dead will live. But they are dust, and can the dust live?"

10. I:12: A Tannaite authority of the house of R. Ishmael taught, "Resurrection is a matter of an argument a fortiori based on the case of a glass utensil. Now if glassware, which is the work of the breath of a mortal man, when broken, can be repaired, A mortal man, who is made by the breath of the Holy One, blessed be he, how much the more so that he can be repaired, in the resurrection of the dead."

11. I:13: A min said to R. Ammi, "You say that the dead will live. But they are dust, and will the dust live?"

12. I:14: A min said to Gebiha, son of Pesisa, a hunchback, "Woe for you! You are guilty! For you say that the dead will live. Those who are alive die, and will those who are dead live?"

5. The Talmud's Union of Halakhah and Aggadah...

B. **TOPICAL APPENDIX ON GEBIHA, SON OF PESISA AND ALEXANDER THE GREAT**

    a.. I:15: Our rabbis have taught on Tannaite authority: When the Africans came to trial with Israel before Alexander of Macedonia, they said to him, "The land of Canaan belongs to us, for it is written, 'The land of Canaan, with the coasts thereof' (Num. 34:2), and Canaan was the father of these men."

    b.. I:16: There was another time, and the Egyptians came to lay claim against Israel before Alexander of Macedonia. They said to him, "Lo, Scripture says, 'And the Lord gave the people favor in the sight of the Egyptians, and they lent them gold and precious stones' (Ex. 12:36). Give us back the silver and gold that you took from us."

    c.. I:17: There was another time, and the children of Ishmael and the children of Keturah came to trial with the Israelites before Alexander of Macedonia. They said to him, "The land of Canaan belongs to us as well as to you, for it is written, 'Now these are the generations of Ishmael, son of Abraham' (Gen. 25:12), and it is written, 'And these are the generations of Isaac, Abraham's son' (Gen. 25:19). Both Ishmael and Isaac have an equal claim on the land, hence so too their descendants."

C. **TOPICAL APPENDIX ON ANTONINUS AND RABBI**

    1. I:18: Antoninus said to Rabbi, "The body and the soul both can exempt themselves from judgment. How so? The body will say, 'The soul is the one that has sinned, for from the day that it left me, lo, I am left like a silent stone in the grave.' And the soul will say, 'The body is the one that sinned. For from the day that I left it, lo, I have been flying about in the air like a bird.'"

    2. I:19: Said Antoninus to Rabbi, "Why does the sun rise in the east and set in the west?"

    3. I:20: Said Antoninus to Rabbi, "At what point is the soul placed in man? Is it at the moment that it is decreed that the person shall be born or when the embryo is formed?"

    4. I:21: And Antoninus said to Rabbi, "At what point does the impulse to do evil take hold of a man? Is it from the moment of creation or from the moment of parturition?"

D. **CONTRASTING VERSES OF SCRIPTURE AND THE DEATH OF DEATH**

    1. I:22: R. Simeon b. Laqish contrasted these two verses: "It is written, 'I will gather them ... with the blind and the lame, the woman with child and her that trail travails with child together'

(Jer. 31:8), and it is written, 'Then shall the lame man leap as a hart and the tongue of the dumb sing, for in the wilderness shall waters break out and streams in the desert' (Is. 35:6). How so will the dead both retain their defects and also be healed? They will rise from the grave bearing their defects and then be healed."

2. I:23: Ulla contrasted these two verses: "It is written, 'He will destroy death forever and the Lord God will wipe away tears from all faces' (Is. 25:9), and it is written, 'For the child shall die a hundred years old ... there shall no more thence an infant of days' (Is. 65:20). There is no contradiction. The one speaks of Israel, the other of idolators." But what do idolators want there in the reestablished state after the resurrection? It is to those concerning whom it is written, "And strangers shall stand and feed your flocks, and the sons of the alien shall be your plowmen and your vine dressers" (Is. 61:5)."

3. I:24: R. Hisda contrasted these two verses: "It is written, 'Then the moon shall be confounded and the sun ashamed, when the Lord of hosts shall reign' (Is 24:23), and it is written, 'Moreover the light of the moon shall be as the light of seven days' (Is 30:26). There is no contradiction. The one refers to the days of the Messiah, the other to the world to come."

4. I:25: Raba contrasted these two verses: "It is written, 'I kill and I make alive' (Deut. 32:"39) and it is written, 'I wound and I heal' (Deut. 32:39). The former implies that one is resurrected just as he was at death, thus with blemishes, and the other implies that at the resurrection all wounds are healed. Said the Holy One, blessed be he, 'What I kill I bring to life,' and then, 'What I have wounded I heal.'"

E. HOW ON THE BASIS OF THE TORAH DO WE KNOW ABOUT THE RESURRECTION OF THE DEAD?

1. I:26: Our rabbis have taught on Tannaite authority: "I kill and I make alive" (Deut. 32:39). Is it possible to suppose that there is death for one person and life for the other, just as the world is accustomed now? Scripture says, "I wound and I heal" (Deut. 32:39). Just as wounding and healing happen to one person, so death and then resurrection happen to one person. From this fact we derive an answer to those who say, "There is no evidence of the resurrection of the dead based on the teachings of the Torah."

2. I:27: It has been taught on Tannaite authority: R. Meir says, "How on the basis of the Torah do we know about the resurrection of the dead?"

3. I:28: Said R. Joshua b. Levi, "How on the basis of Scripture may we prove the resurrection of the dead?

5. The Talmud's Union of Halakhah and Aggadah...

4. I:29: Said R. Judah said Rab, "Whoever withholds a teaching of law from a disciple is as if he steals the inheritance of his fathers from him, for it is said, 'Moses commanded us Torah, even the inheritance of the congregation of Jacob' (Deut. 33:4). It is an inheritance destined for all Israel from the six days of creation."
5. I:30: Said R. Sheshet, "Whoever teaches Torah in this world will have the merit of teaching it in the world to come."
6. I:31: Said Raba, "How on the basis of the Torah do we find evidence for the resurrection of the dead?"
7. I:32: Said R. Eleazar, "Every authority who leads the community serenely will have the merit of leading them in the world to come, as it is said, 'For he who has mercy on them shall lead them, even by springs of water shall he guide them' (Is. 49:10)."
8. I:33: Said R. Tabi said R. Josiah, "What is the meaning of this verse of Scripture: 'The grave and the barren womb and the earth that is not filled by water' (Prov. 30:16). What has the grave to do with the womb? It is to say to you, just as the womb takes in and gives forth, so Sheol takes in and gives forth."
9. I:34: A Tannaite authority of the house of Elisha taught, "The righteous whom the Holy One, blessed be he, is going to resurrect will not revert to dust, for it is said, 'And it shall come to pass that he that is left in Zion and he that remains in Jerusalem shall be called holy, even everyone that is written among the living in Jerusalem, (Is. 4:3). Just as the Holy One lives forever, so they shall live forever." The passage concludes with the following, which accounts for the inclusion of I.35's statement on Nebuchadnezzar, thus the entire composite on Hananiah, Mishael, and Azariah: And said R. Yohanan, "From the river Eshel to Rabbath is the valley of Dura. For when Nebuchadnezzar, that wicked man, exiled Israel, there were young men who outshone the sun in their beauty. Chaldean women would see them and reach orgasm from the mere gaze. They told their husbands and their husbands told the king. The king ordered them killed. Still, the wives would reach orgasm merely from laying eyes on the corpses. The king gave an order and they trampled the corpses beyond all recognition."
    a. I:35: Our rabbis have taught on Tannaite authority: When Nebuchadnezzar, the wicked man, cast Hananiah, Mishael, and Azariah, into the fiery furnace, the Holy One, blessed be he, said to Ezekiel, "Go and raise the dead in the valley of Dura." When he had raised them, the bones came and smacked that wicked man in his face. He said, "What are

these things?" They said to him, "The friend of these is raising the dead in the valley of Dura." He then said, "'How great are his signs, and how mighty his wonders. His kingdom is an everlasting kingdom, and his dominion is from generation to generation' (Dan. 3:23)."

F. TOPICAL APPENDIX ON HANANIAH, MISHAEL, AND AZARIAH

I. I:36: Our rabbis have taught on Tannaite authority: Six miracles were done on that day, and these are they:

II. I:37: A Tannaite authority of the house of R. Eliezer b. Jacob taught, "Even in time of danger a person should not pretend that he does not hold his high office, For it is said, 'Then these men were bound in their coats, their hose, and their other garments' (Dan. 3:21). These were garments specially worn by men in their exalted position, and they did not doff them though cast into the furnace."

III. I:38: Said R. Yohanan, "The righteous are greater than ministering angels. For it is said, 'He answered and said, Lo, I see four men loose, walking in the midst of the fire, and they are not hurt, and the form of the fourth is like the son of God' (Dan. 3:25). Thus the angel is mentioned last, as being least esteemed."

IV. I:39: Said R. Tanhum bar Hanilai, "When Hananiah, Mishael, and Azariah went out of the fiery furnace, all the nations of the world came and slapped the enemies of Israel — that is, Israel — on their faces."

V. I:40: Said R. Samuel bar Nahmani said R. Jonathan, "What is the meaning of the verse of Scripture, 'I said, I will go up to the palm tree, I will take hold of the boughs thereof' (Song 7:9)?'I said I will go up to the palm tree' refers to Israel. But now 'I grasped' only one bough, namely, Hananiah, Mishael and Azariah."

VI. I:41: And said R. Yohanan, "What is the meaning of the verse of Scripture, 'I saw by night, and behold a man riding upon a red horse, and he stood among the myrtle trees that were in the bottom' (Zech. 1:8).? What is the meaning of, 'I saw by night'? The Holy One blessed be he, sought to turn the entire world into night. 'And behold, a man riding' — 'man' refers only to the Holy One, blessed be he, as it is said, 'The Lord is a man of war, the Lord is his name' (Ex. 15:3). 'On a red horse' — the Holy One, blessed be he, sought to turn the entire world to blood. When, however, he saw Hananiah,

Mishael, and Azariah, he cooled off, as it is said, 'And he stood among the myrtle trees that were in the deep.'"

VII. I:42: The rabbis Hananiah, Mishael, and Azariah — where did they go?

VIII. I:43: Our rabbis have taught on Tannaite authority: There were three who were involved in that scheme to keep Daniel out of the furnace: the Holy One, blessed be he, Daniel, and Nebuchadnezzar.

IX. I:44: "Thus says the Lord of hosts, the God of Israel, of Ahab, son of Kolaiah, and of Zedekiah, son of Maaseiah, who prophesy a lie to you in my name" (Jer. 29:21) And it is written, "And of them shall be taken up a curse by all the captivity of Judah who are in Babylonia, saying, The Lord make you like Zedekiah and like Ahab, whom the king of Babylonia roasted in fire" (Jer. 29:22). What is said is not "whom he burned in fire" but "whom he roasted in fire."

X. I:45: "Because they have committed villainy in Israel and have committed adultery with their neighbors' wives" (Jer. 29:23): What did they do? They went to Nebuchadnezzar's daughter. Ahab said to her, "Thus said the Lord, 'Give yourself to Zedekiah.'"

XI. I:46: Said R. Tanhum, "In Sepphoris, bar Qappara interpreted the following verse: 'These six grains of barley gave he to me' (Ruth 3:17). What are the six of barley? If we should say that they were actually six of barley, was it the way of Boaz to give out a gift of only six barley grains? Rather it must have been six seahs of barley? And is it the way of a woman to carry six seahs? Rather, this formed an omen to her that six sons are destined to come forth from her, each of whom would receive six blessings, and these are they: David, the Messiah, Daniel, Hananiah, Mishael, and Azariah. David, as it is written, 'Then answered one of the servants and said, Behold I have seen the son of Jesse, the Bethlehemite, who is cunning in playing and a mighty, valiant man, and a man of war, and understanding in matters, and a handsome man, and the Lord is with him' (1 Sam. 16:18). The six epithets, viz., cunning in playing, mighty, valiant, etc., are regarded as blessings applicable to each of the six persons mentioned."

XII. I:47: "Now among these were of the children of Judah, Daniel, Hananiah, Mishael, and Azariah" (Dan. 1:6): Said R. Eleazar, "All of them came from the children of Judah." And R. Samuel bar Nahmani said, "Daniel came from the children of Judah, but Hananiah, Mishael, and Azariah came from the other tribes."

XIII. I:48: "And of your sons which shall issue from you, which you shall beget, shall they take away, and they shall be eunuchs in the palace of the king of Babylonia" (2 Kgs. 20:18): What are these "eunuchs"? Rab said, "Literally, eunuchs." And R. Hanina said, "The sense is that idolatry was castrated i.e. made sterile in their time." In the view of him who has said that idolatry was castrated in their time, that is in line with the verse of Scripture, "And there is no hurt in them" (Dan. 3:25). But in the view of him who says that "eunuch" is in its literal sense, what is the meaning of, "And there is no hurt in them" (Dan. 3:25) Since they had been castrated? It is that the fire did them no injury.

XIV. I:49: Now since whatever concerns Ezra was stated by Nehemiah b. Hachlia, what is the reason that the book was not called by his name? Said R. Jeremiah bar Abba, "It is because he took pride in himself, as it is written, 'Think up on me for good, my God' (Neh. 5:19)." David also made such a statement, "Remember me, Lord, with the favor that you bear for your people, visit me with your salvation" (Ps. 106:4). It was supplication that David sought. R. Joseph said, "It was because Nehemiah had spoken disparagingly about his predecessors, as it is said, 'But the former governors who had been before me were chargeable unto the people and had taken of them bread and wine, beside forty shekels of silver' (Neh. 5:15). Furthermore, he spoke in this way even of Daniel, who was greater than he was." And how do we know that Daniel was greater than he was?

G. THE MESSIAH. PHARAOH, SENNACHERIB, HEZEKIAH, AND OTHER PLAYERS IN THE MESSIANIC DRAMA

1. I:50: Of the increase of his government and peace there shall be no end" (Is. 9:6): R. Tanhum said, "In Sepphoris, Bar Qappara expounded this verse as follows: 'On what account is every M in the middle of a word open, but the one in the word "increase" is closed? 'The Holy One, blessed be he, proposed to make

5. The Talmud's Union of Halakhah and Aggadah...

Hezekiah Messiah, and Sennacherib into Gog and Magog. 'The attribute of justice said before the Holy One, blessed be he, "Lord of the world, Now if David, king of Israel, who recited how many songs and praises before you, you did not make Messiah, Hezekiah, for whom you have done all these miracles, and who did not recite a song before you, surely should not be made Messiah."

2. I:51: "The burden of Dumah. He calls to me out of Seir, Watchman, what of the night? Watchman, what of the night?" (Is. 21:11): Said R. Yohanan, "That angel who is appointed over the souls is named Dumah. All the souls gathered to Dumah, and said to him, '"Watchman, what of the night? Watchman, what of the night?' (Is. 21:11). Said the watchman, 'The morning comes and also the night, if you will inquire, inquire, return, come' (Is. 21:11)."

3. I:52: A Tannaite authority in the name of R. Pappias said, "It was a shame for Hezekiah and his associates that they did not recite a song, until the earth opened and said a song, as it is said, 'From the uttermost part of the earth have we hard songs, even glory to the righteous' (Is. 24:16)."

   a. I:53: "And Jethro rejoiced" (Ex. 18:9) Rab and Samuel — Rab said, "It was that he passed a sharp knife across his flesh circumcising himself." And Samuel said, "All his flesh became goose-pimples because of the destruction of the Egyptians."

4. I:54: "Therefore shall the Lord, the Lord of hosts, send among his fat ones leanness" (Is. 10:16): What is "among his fat ones leanness"? Said the Holy One, blessed be he, "Let Hezekiah come, who has eight names, and exact punishment from Sennacherib, who has eight names."

5. I:55: "And beneath his glory shall he kindle a burning like the burning of a fire" (Is. 10:16): Said R. Yohanan, "Under his glory, but not actually his glory."

6. I:56: A Tannaite authority in the name of R. Joshua b. Qorhah taught, "Since Pharaoh blasphemed personally, the Holy One, blessed be he, exacted punishment from him personally. Since Sennacherib blasphemed through a messenger, the Holy One, blessed be he, exacted punishment from him through a messenger."

7. I:57: R. Hanina b. Pappa contrasted two verses: "It is written, 'I will enter the height of his border' (Is. 37:24), and it is further written, 'I will enter into the lodgings of his borders' (2 Kgs. 19:23). Said that wicked man, 'First I shall destroy the lower dwelling, and afterward I shall destroy the upper dwelling."

8. I:58: Said R. Joshua b. Levi, "What is the meaning of the verse of Scripture, 'Am I now come up without the Lord against this place to destroy it? The Lord said to me, Go up against this land and destroy it' (2 Kgs. 18:25). What is the sense of the passage? He had heard the prophet, who had said, 'Since this people refuses the waters of Shiloah that go softly and rejoice in Rezina and Ramaliah's son, now therefore behold the Lord brings up upon them the waters of the river, strong and many, even the king of Assyria and all his glory, and he shall come up over all his channels and go over all his banks' (Is. 8:6). This was understood by Sennacherib as an order to possess Jerusalem."

9. I:59: Said R. Yohanan, "What is the meaning of this verse: 'The curse of the Lord is in the house of the wicked, but he blesses the habitation of the just' (Prov. 3:33)? 'The curse of the Lord is in the house of the wicked' refers to Pekah, son of Remaliah, who would eat forty seahs of pigeons for desert. 'But he blesses the habitation of the just' refers to Hezekiah, king of Judea, who would eat a litra of vegetables for a whole meal."

10. I:60: "Now therefore behold, the Lord brings up upon them the waters of the river, strong and many, even the king of Assyria and all his glory" (Is. 8:7). And it is written, "And he shall pass through Judea, he shall overflow and go over, he shall reach even to the neck" (Is. 8:8). Then why was Sennacherib punished?

11. I:61: What is the meaning of this verse: "When aforetime the land of Zebulun and the land of Naphtali lightened its burden, but in later times it was made heavy by the way of the sea, beyond Jordan, in Galilee of the nations" (Is. 8:23)? It was not like the early generations, who made the yoke of the Torah light for themselves, but the later generations, who made the yoke of the Torah heavy for themselves. And these were worthy that a miracle should be done for them, just as was done for those who passed through the sea and trampled over the Jordan.

12. I:62: "After these things, and the truth thereof, Sennacherib, king of Assyria, came and entered Judea and encamped against the fortified cities and thought to win them for himself" (2 Chr. 32:1): Such a recompense to Hezekiah for such a gift? The previous verse relates that Hezekiah turned earnestly to the service of God. Was then Sennacherib's invasion his just reward?

13. I:63: "And it shall come to pass in that day that his burden shall be taken away from off your shoulders and his yoke from off your neck, and the yoke shall be destroyed because of the oil" (Is. 10:27): Said R. Isaac Nappaha, "The yoke of Sennacherib

will be destroyed because of the oil of Hezekiah, which he would kindle in the synagogues and school houses. What did Hezekiah do? He affixed a sword at the door of the school house and said, 'Whoever does not take up study of the Torah will be pierced by this sword.' They searched from Dan to Beer Sheba and found no ignoramus, from Gabbath to Antipatris and found no boy or girl, no man or woman, not expert in the laws of uncleanness and cleanness."

14. I:64: "And your spoil shall be gathered like the gathering of a caterpillar" (Is. 33:4): Said the prophet to Israel, "Gather your spoil." They said to him, "Is it for individual spoil or for sharing?" He said to them, "'Like the gathering of a caterpillar' (Is. 33:4): Just as in the gathering of a caterpillar it is each one for himself, so in your spoil it is each one for himself."

15. I:65: Said R. Huna, "That wicked man Sennacherib made ten marches that day, as it is said, 'He is come to Aiath, he is passed at Migron, at Michmash he has laid up his carriages, they are gone over the passage, they have taken up their lodgings at Geba, Ramah is afraid, Gibeah of Saul is fled, Lift up your voice, O daughter of Gallim, cause it to be heard to Laish, O poor Anathoth, Madmenah is removed, the inhabitants of Gebim gather themselves to flee' (Is. 10:28-31)."

16. I:66: What is the meaning of the statement, "As yet shall be halt at Nob that day" (Is. 10:32)? Said R. Huna, "That day alone remained for the punishment of the sin committed at Nob Sam. 22:17-19. When the priests of Nob were massacred. God set a term for punishment, of which that day was the last.

17. I:67: "And Ishbi-benob, who was of the sons of the giant, the weight of whose spear weighed three hundred shekels of brass in weight, being girded with a new sword, thought to have slain David" (2 Sam. 21:16): What is the sense of "Ishbi-be-nob"? Said R. Judah said Rab, "It was a man ish who came on account of the matter of the sin committed at Nob. Said the Holy One, blessed be he, to David, 'How long will the sin committed against Nob be concealed in your hand. On your account, Nob was put to death, the city of priests, on your account, Doeg the Edomite was sent into exile; on your account, Saul and his three sons were killed. 'Do you want you descendents to be wiped out, or do you want to be handed over into the power of an enemy?' He said to him, 'Lord of the world, It is better that I be handed over to an enemy but that my descendents not be wiped out.'"

    a. I:68: Our rabbis have taught on Tannaite authority: For three did the earth fold up to make their journey quicker: Eliezer,

Abraham's servant, Jacob our father, and Abishai b. Zeruiah. As to Abishai, son of Zeruiah, it is as we have just said. As to Eliezer, Abraham's servant, it is written, "And I came this day to the well" (Gen. 24:42), meaning that that very day he had set out. As to Jacob, our father, as it is written, "And Jacob went out from Beer Sheba and went to Haran" (Gen. 28:10), and it is said, "And he lighted upon a certain place and tarried there all night, because the sun had set" (Gen. 28:11).

18. I:69: And how do we know that the seed of David ceased
19. I:70: Said R. Judah said Rab, "The wicked Sennacherib came against them with forty-five thousand men, sons of kings seated on golden chariots, with their concubines and whores, and with eighty thousand mighty soldiers, garbed in coats of mail, and sixty thousand swordsmen running before him, and the rest cavalry. And so they came against Abraham, and in the age to come so they will come with Gog and Magog."
20. I:71: It was taught on Tannaite authority: The first ones crossed by swimming, as it is said, "He shall overflow and go over" (Is. 8:8). The middle ones crossed standing up, as it is said, "He shall reach even to the neck" (Is. 8:8). The last group brought up the dirt of the river with their feet and so found no water in the river to drink, so that they had to bring them water from some other place, which they drank, as it is said, "I have dug and drunk water" (Is. 37:25).
21. I:72: How did the angel smite the army?
22. I:73: How many of Sennacherib's army remained?
23. I:74: Said R. Abbahu, "Were it not that a verse of Scripture is explicitly spelled out, it would not have been possible to say it: For it is written, 'In the same day shall the Lord shave with a razor that is hired, namely, by the riverside, by the king of Assyria, the head and the hair of the feet, and it shall consume the beard' (Is. 7:20. The Holy One, blessed be he, came and appeared before Sennacherib as an old man. He said to him, 'When you go against the kings of east and west, whose sons you brought and saw killed, what will you say to them?'"
    a. I:75: "And he fought against them, he and his servants, by night, and smote them" (Gen. 14:15): Said R. Yohanan, "That angel who was assigned to Abraham was named 'Night,' as it is said, 'Let the day perish wherein I was born and the Night which said, There is a man-child conceived' (Job 3:3). The verse, Gen. 14:15, is translated, and Night fought on

5. The Talmud's Union of Halakhah and Aggadah...

their behalf, he and his....'" Inserted because of the concluding statement: Said R. Yohanan, "When that righteous man came to Dan, he grew weak. He foresaw that the children of his children were destined to commit acts of idolatry in Dan, as it is said, 'And he set the one in Beth El, and the other he put in Dan' (1 Kgs. 12:29). And also that wicked man Nebuchadnezzar did not grow strong until he reached Dan, as it is said, 'From Dan the snorting of his horses was heard' (Jer. 8:16)."

25. I:76: Said R. Zira, "Even though R. Judah b. Beterah sent word from Nisibis, 'Pay heed to an elder who has forgotten his learning through not fault of his own and to cut the jugular veins in slaughtering a beast, in accord with the view of R. Judah, 'and take heed of the sons of the ordinary folk, for from them too will Torah go forth,' for such a matter as the following we may convey matters to them and not refrain from teaching this lesson: '"You are righteous, Lord, when I please with you, yet let met talk to thee of your judgments, wherefore does the way of the wicked prosper? Wherefore are all they happy who deal very treacherously? You have planted them, yes, they have taken root, they grow, yes, they bring forth fruit" (Jer. 12:1-2).

26. I:77: What is the meaning of the fact that Merodach-Baladan is called "the son of Baladan"? They say: Baladan was king, and his appearance changed into that of a dog, so his son sat on the throne. When he would sign a document, he would write his name and the name of his father, "King Baladan."

27. I:78: Said Raba, "It was bearing three hundred mules loaded with iron axes that could break iron that Nebuchadnezzar sent Nebuzaradan. All of them broke on one gate of Jerusalem, as it is said, 'And now they attack its gate together; with axes and hammers they hit it' (Ps. 74:6). He wanted to go back. He said, 'I am afraid that they might do to me as they did to Sennacherib. A voice came forth: 'Leaper son of a leaper, leap, Nebuzaradan! The time has come for the sanctuary to be destroyed and the palace burned.'"

    a. I:79: Our rabbis have taught on Tannaite authority: Naaman was a resident proselyte. Nebuzaradan was a righteous proselyte. Grandsons of Sisera studied Torah in Jerusalem. Grandsons of Sennacherib taught Torah in public.

28. I:80: Said Ulla, "Ammon and Moab were bad neighbors of Jerusalem. When they heard the prophets prophesying the destruction of Jerusalem, they sent word to Nebuchadnezzar, 'Go

out and come here.' He said, 'I am afraid that they will do to me what they did to those who came before me.' They sent to him, '"For the man is not at home" (Prov. 7:19), and "man" can refer only to the Holy One, blessed be he, as it is said, "The Lord is a man of war" (Ex. 15:3).' He replied, 'He is nearby and he will come.' They sent to him, '"He has gone on a far journey" (Prov. 7:19).' He sent to them, 'There are righteous men there, who will pray for mercy and bring him back."'

H. WHEN WILL THE MESSIAH COME?

1. I:81: Said R. Nahman to R. Isaac, "Have you heard when the son of 'the fallen one' will come?" He said to him, "Who is the son of 'the fallen one'?" He said to him, "It is the Messiah." "Do you call the Messiah 'the son of the fallen one'?" He said to him, "Yes, for it is written, 'On that day I will raise up the tabernacle of David, the fallen one' (Amos 9:11)."

2. I:82: Our rabbis have taught on Tannaite authority: The seven year cycle in which the son of David will come: As to the first one, the following verse of Scripture will be fulfilled: "And I will cause it to rain upon one city and not upon another" (Amos 4:7). As to the second year, the arrows of famine will be sent forth. As to the third, there will be a great famine, in which men, women, and children will die, pious men and wonder-workers alike, and the Torah will be forgotten by those that study it. As to the fourth year, there will be plenty which is no plenty. As to the fifth year, there will be great prosperity, and people will eat, drink, and rejoice, and the Torah will be restored to those that study it. As to the sixth year, there will be rumors. As to the seventh year, there will be wars.

3. I:83: It has been taught on Tannaite authority: R. Judah says, "In the generation in which the son of David will come, the gathering place will be for prostitution, Galilee will be laid waste, Gablan will be made desolate, and the men of the frontier will go about from town to town, and none will take pity on them; and the wisdom of scribes will putrefy; and those who fear sin will be rejected; and the truth will be herded away (M. Sot. 9:15AA-GG).

   a. I:84: Said Raba, "To begin with I had supposed that there is no truth in the world. One of the rabbis, R. Tabut by name (and some say, R. Tabyomi by name), who would not go back on his word even though people gave him all the treasures of the world, said to me that one time he happened to come to a place called Truth."

5. The Talmud's Union of Halakhah and Aggadah...

4. I:85: It has been taught on Tannaite authority: **R. Nehorai says, "In the generation in which the son of David will come, children will shame elders, and elders will stand up before children. 'The daughter rises up against the mother, and the daughter-in-law against her mother-in-law' (Mic. 7:6). The face of the generation is the face of a dog, and a son is not ashamed before his father" (M. Sot. 9:15HH-KK).**

5. I:86: It has been taught on Tannaite authority: **R. Nehemiah says, "In the generation in which the son of David will come, presumption increases, and dearth increases, and the vine gives its fruit and wine at great cost. The government turns to heresy, and there is no reproof" (M. Sot. 9:15W-Z).**

6. I:87: Our rabbis have taught on Tannaite authority: "For the Lord shall judge his people and repent himself of his servants, when he sees that their power has gone, and there is none shut up or left" (Deut. 32:36). The son of David will come only when traitors are many. Another matter: Only when disciples are few. Another matter: Only when a penny will not be found in anyone's pocket.

7. I:88: Said R. Qattina, "The world will exist for six thousand years and be destroyed for one thousand, as it is said, 'And the Lord alone shall be exalted in that day' (Is. 2:11)." Abbayye said, "It will be desolate for two thousand years, as it is said, 'After two days will he revive us, in the third day, he will raise us up and we shall live in his sight' (Hos. 6:2)."

8. I:89: A Tannaite authority of the house of Elijah said, "For six thousand years the world will exist. For two thousand it will be desolate, two thousand years will be the time of Torah, and two thousand years will be the days of the Messiah."

9. I:90: Said Elijah to R. Sala the Pious, "The world will last for no fewer than eighty-five Jubilees of fifty years each, and the son of David will come in the last one."

10. I:91: R. Hanan, son of Tahalipa, sent to R. Joseph, "I came across a man who had in hand a scroll, written in Assyrian block letters in the holy language. I said to him, 'Where did you get this?' He said to me, 'I was employed in the Roman armies, and I found it in the Roman archives.' In the scroll it is written that after four thousand two hundred ninety-two years from the creation of the world, the world will be an orphan. As to the years to follow in some there will be wars of the great dragons, and in some, wars of Gog and Magog, and the rest will be the days of the Messiah. And the Holy One, blessed be he, will renew his world only after seven thousand years."

11. I:92: It has been taught on Tannaite authority: R. Nathan says, "This verse of Scripture pierces to the depth: 'For the vision is yet for an appointed time, but at the end it shall speak and not lie; though he tarry, wait for him; because it will surely come, it will not tarry' (Hab. 2:3)."

12. I:93: What is the meaning of the verse, "But at the end it shall speak and not lie" (Hab. 2:3)? Said R. Samuel bar Nahmani said R. Jonathan, " Reading the verse as, 'He will blast him who calculates the end,' blasted be the bones of those who calculate the end when the Messiah will come. For they might say, 'Since the end has come and he has not come, he will not come.' Rather, wait for him, as it is said, 'Though he tarry, wait for him' (Hab. 2:3)."

13. I:94: Said Abbayye, "There are in the world never fewer than thirty-six righteous men, who look upon the face of the Presence of God every day, for it is said, 'Happy are those who wait for him' (Is. 30:18), and the numerical value of the letters in the word 'for him' is thirty-six."

14. I:95: Said Rab, "All of the ends have passed, and the matter now depends only on repentance and good deeds." And Samuel said, "It is sufficient for a mourner to remain firm in his mourning."

15. I:96: And said R. Abba, "You have no indication of the end more openly stated than the following, as it is said: 'But you, O Mountains of Israel, shall shoot forth your branches and yield your fruit to my people, Israel, for they are at hand to come' (Ez. 36:8)."

16. I:97: Said R. Hanina, "The son of David will come only when a fish will be sought for a sick person and not be found, as it is said, 'Then I will make their waters deep and cause their rivers to run like oil' (Ez. 32:14), and it is written, 'In that day I will cause the horn of the house of Israel to sprout forth' (Ez. 29:21)." Said R. Hama bar Hanina, "The son of David will come only when the rule over Israel by the least of the kingdoms will come to an end, as it is said, 'He shall both cut off the springs with pruning hooks and take away and cut down the branches' (Is. 18:5), and further: 'In that time shall the present be brought to the Lord of hosts of a people that is scattered and peeled' (Is. 18:7)."

17. I:98: Said Ulla, "Jerusalem will be redeemed only through righteousness, as it is written, 'Zion shall be redeemed with judgment and her converts with righteousness' (Is. 1:27)." Said R. Pappa, "If the arrogant end in Israel, the Magi will end in Iran, if the judges end in Israel, the rulers of thousands will come

5. The Talmud's Union of Halakhah and Aggadah...

to an end in Iran. If the arrogant end in Israel, the magi will end in Iran, as it is written, 'And I will purely purge away your haughty ones and take away all your tin' (Is. 1:25). If judges end in Israel, the rulers of thousands will come to an end in Iran, as it is written, 'The Lord has taken away your judgments, he has cast out your enemy' (Zeph. 3:15)."

18. I:99: Said R. Yohanan, "If you see a generation growing less and less, hope for him more and more, as it is said, 'And the afflicted people will you save' (2 Sam. 22:28)." Said R. Yohanan, "If you see a generation over which many troubles flow like a river, hope for him, as it is written, 'When the enemy shall come in like a flood, the spirit of the Lord shall lift up a standard against him' (Is. 59:19), followed by: 'And the redeemer shall come to Zion' (Is. 59:20)."

19. I:100: Said R. Alexandri, "R. Joshua b. Levi contrasted verses as follows: It is written; "in its time will the Messiah come," and it is also written; "I the Lord will hasten it." What is the meaning of the contrast? If the Israelites have merit, I will hasten it, if they do not, the messiah will come in due course."

20. I:101: Said King Shapur to Samuel, "You say that the Messiah will come on an ass which is a humble way. Come and I shall send him a white horse that I have."

21. I:102: . Joshua b. Levi found Elijah standing at the door of the burial vault of R. Simeon b. Yohai. He said to him, "Am I going to come to the world to come?" He said to him, "If this master wants." Said R. Joshua b. Levi, "Two did I see, but a third voice did I hear." He said to him, "When is the Messiah coming?" He said to him, "Go and ask him."

22. I:103: His disciples asked R. Yosé b. Qisma, "When is the son of David coming?"

23. I:104: Said Rab, "The son of David will come only when the monarchy of Rome will spread over Israel for nine months."

24. I:105: Said Ulla, "Let him come, but may I not see him." Said Rabba, "Let him come, but may I not see him." R. Joseph said, "May he come, and may I have the merit of sitting in the shade of the dung of his ass."

25. I:106: So said R. Yohanan, "Let him come, but let me not see him."

26. I:107: Said R. Giddal said Rab, "The Israelites are going to eat and not starve in the years of the Messiah."

27. I:108: Said Rab, "The world was created only for David." And Samuel said, "For Moses." And R. Yohanan said, "For the Messiah."

28. I:109: Said R. Nahman, "If he is among the living, he is such as I, as it is said, 'And their nobles shall be of themselves and their governors shall proceed from the midst of them' (Jer. 30:21)." Said Rab, "If he is among the living, he is such as our Holy Rabbi Judah the Patriarch, and if he is among the dead, he is such as Daniel, the most desirable man."

29. I:110: R. Simlai interpreted the following verse: "What is the meaning of that which is written, 'Woe to you who desire the day of the Lord! to what end is it for you? the day of the Lord is darkness and not light' (Amos 5:18)? The matter may be compared to the case of the cock and the bat who were waiting for light. The cock said to the bat, 'I am waiting for the light, for the light belongs to me, but what do you need light for?' That is in line with what a min said to R. Abbahu, "When is the Messiah coming?" He said to him, "When darkness covers those men."

30. I:111: It has been taught on Tannaite authority: R. Eliezer says, "The days of the Messiah will last forty years, as it is said, 'Forty years long shall I take hold of the generation' (Ps. 95:10)." R. Eliezer b. Azariah says, "Seventy years, as it is said, 'And it shall come to pass in that day that Tyre shall be forgotten seventy years, according to the days of one king' (Is. 23:15)."

31. I:112: R. Hillel says, "Israel will have no Messiah, for they consumed him in the time of Hezekiah."

32. I:113: A further teaching on Tannaite authority: R. Eliezer says, "The days of the Messiah will last for forty years. Here it is written, 'And he afflicted you and made you hunger and fed you with manna' (Deut. 8:3), and elsewhere: 'Make us glad according to the days forty years in the wilderness in which you have afflicted us' (Ps. 90:15)." R. Dosa says, "Four hundred years. Here it is written, 'And they shall serve them and they shall afflict them four hundred years' (Gen. 15:13), and elsewhere: 'Make us glad according to the days wherein you have afflicted us' (Ps. 90:15)."

33. I:114: Said R. Hiyya bar Abba said R. Yohanan, "All of the prophets prophesied only concerning the days of the Messiah. But as to the world to come thereafter: 'Eye has not seen, O Lord, beside you, what he has prepared for him who waits for him' (Is. 64:3)."

We find a sustained effort at recasting the Mishnah's topic by introducing themes that the Mishnah either omits altogether or treats in a casual way. These emerge in the sequence outlined here: the death of death; the coming of the Messiah — past time; the coming of the Messiah — future time; the special case of Hezekiah and the pertinence of the book of Lamentations. Here in a single set of composites we find introduced a set of propositions concerning the Messiah and Israel's history that the Mishnah has neglected.

The Mishnah, after all, has focused upon private persons — specific kings and commoners who have lost the world to come. The Gemara, by contrast, introduces the dimension of the Israelite corporate community seen whole. The Mishnah tells us how individuals lose out, e.g., by denying that the Torah itself teaches that the dead will be raised. The Gemara turns to the more profound question of the death of death, which itself then comes as the prologue to the advent of the Messiah. As though to underscore the main point — the issue is Israel the holy people, not merely individual players in Israelite life — the exegesis of Lamentations is inserted, whole and in no clear connection to what has preceded.

The result of this analysis leaves no doubt that the framers of the Gemara have both commented upon the Mishnah in a rich and remarkably profound way but also recast the context in which the Mishnah is to be received and understood. The Gemara truly forms the re-presentation of the Mishnah. And what the Gemara's framers find self-evident in the exposition of the Mishnah's statements that the Mishnah's authors treated casually or not at all speaks for itself.

IV. THE AGGADAH OF SANHEDRIN: THE MISHNAH'S PROVISION OF RESURRECTION AND WHO IS EXCLUDED. MISHNAH-TRACTATE SANHEDRIN CHAPTER ELEVEN, BAVLI SANHEDRIN 11:1/I.2-14/90B-91B

The Aggadic component of Sanhedrin holds that death does not mark the end of the individual human life, nor exile the last stop in the journey of Holy Israel. Israelites will live in the age, or the world, to come, all Israel in the Land of Israel; and Israel will comprehend all who know the one true God. So far as the individual is concerned, beyond the grave, at a determinate moment, the Israelite individual [1] rises from the grave in resurrection, [2] is judged, and [3] enjoys the world to come. For the entirety of Israel, congruently: all Israel participates in the resurrection, which takes place in the Land of Israel, and enters the world to come. The last things are to be known from the first. In the just plan of creation Adam was meant to live in Eden, and Israel in the Land of Israel in time without end. The restoration will bring about that long and tragically-postponed perfection of the world order, sealing the demonstration of the justice of God's plan for creation. Risen from the dead, having atoned through death, the Israelite will be judged in accord with his deeds. The people, Israel, for its part, when it repents and conforms its will to God's, recovers its Eden. So the consequences of rebellion and sin having been overcome, the struggle of man's will and God's word having been resolved, God's original plan will be realized at the last.

The components of the doctrine fit together, in a logical order. [1] In a predictable application of the governing principle of measure for measure, those who do not believe in the resurrection of the dead will be punished by being denied what they do not accept. Some few others bear the same fate. [2] To be Israel means to rise from the grave, and that applies to all Israelites. That is to say, the given of the condition of Israel is that the entire holy people will enter the world to come, which is to say, will enjoy the resurrection of the dead and eternal life. "Israel" then is anticipated to be the people of eternity. [3] Excluded from the category of resurrection and the world to come, then, are only those who by their own sins have denied themselves that benefit. These are those that deny that the teaching of the world to come derives from the Torah, or who deny that the Torah comes from God, or hedonists. Exegesis of Scripture also yields the names of three kings who will not be resurrected, as well as four commoners; also specified generations: the flood, the dispersion, and Sodom, the generation of the wilderness, the party of Korah, and the Ten Tribes:

Mishnah-tractate Sanhedrin 11:1[3]

A. All Israelites have a share in the world to come,
B. as it is said, "Your people also shall be all righteous, they shall inherit the land forever; the branch of my planting, the work of my hands, that I may be glorified" (Is. 60:21).

Matching the definition of the gentile as idolater, this single statement serves better than any other to define "Israel" in the Talmud. Israel is comprised by all those who will live forever: "All those who have a share in the world to come are Israel." To live forever is to stand in judgment, and how idolaters can stand in judgment is hardly clear. The upshot is, all that sector of humanity that knows and worships God looks forward to life eternal. Now we forthwith take up exceptions, first, Israelites, next, gentiles (which bears the clear implication that some gentiles will live forever too):

C. And these are the ones who have no portion in the world to come:
D. He who says, the resurrection of the dead is a teaching which does not derive from the Torah, and the Torah does not come from Heaven; and an Epicurean.
E. R. Aqiba says, "Also: He who reads in heretical books,
F. "and he who whispers over a wound and says, 'I will put none of the diseases upon you which I have put on the Egyptians, for I am the Lord who heals you' (Ex. 15:26)."
G. Abba Saul says, "Also: He who pronounces the divine Name as it is spelled out."

From classes of persons, we turn to specified individuals who are denied a place within Israel and entry in the world to come; all but one are Israelites, and the exception, Balaam, has a special relation to Israel, as the gentile prophet who came to curse but ended with a blessing:

5. The Talmud's Union of Halakhah and Aggadah...

MISHNAH-TRACTATE SANHEDRIN 11:2

A. Three kings and four ordinary folk have no portion in the world to come.
B. Three kings: Jeroboam, Ahab, and Manasseh.
C. R. Judah says, "Manasseh has a portion in the world to come,
D. "since it is said, 'And he prayed to him and he was entreated of him and heard his supplication and brought him again to Jerusalem into his kingdom' (2 Chr. 33:13)."
E. They said to him, "To his kingdom he brought him back, but to the life of the world to come he did not bring him back."
F. Four ordinary folk: Balaam, Doeg, Ahitophel, and Gehazi.

Then come entire generations of gentiles before Abraham, who might have been considered for eternal life outside of the framework of God's self-manifestation, first to Abraham, then in the Torah. These are the standard sets, the Generation of the Flood, the Generation of the Dispersion, and the Men of Sodom:

MISHNAH-TRACTATE SANHEDRIN 11:3

A. The generation of the flood has no share in the world to come,
B. and they shall not stand in the judgment,
C. since it is written, "My spirit shall not judge with man forever" (Gen. 6:3)
D. neither judgment nor spirit.
E. The generation of the dispersion has no share in the world to come,
F. since it is said, "So the Lord scattered them abroad from there upon the face of the whole earth" (Gen. 11:8).
G. "So the Lord scattered them abroad" — in this world,
H. "and the Lord scattered them from there" — in the world to come.
I. The men of Sodom have no portion in the world to come,
J. since it is said, "Now the men of Sodom were wicked and sinners against the Lord exceedingly" (Gen. 13:13)
K. "Wicked" — in this world,
L. "And sinners" — in the world to come.
M. But they will stand in judgment.
N. R. Nehemiah says, "Both these and those will not stand in judgment,
O. 'for it is said, 'Therefore the wicked shall not stand in judgment [108A], nor sinners in the congregation of the righteous' (Ps. 1:5)
P. 'Therefore the wicked shall not stand in judgment' — this refers to the generation of the flood.
Q. 'Nor sinners in the congregation of the righteous' — this refers to the men of Sodom."
R. They said to him, "They will not stand in the congregation of the righteous, but they will stand in the congregation of the sinners."
S. The spies have no portion in the world to come,

T. as it is said, "Even those men who brought up an evil report of the land died by the plague before the Lord" (Num. 14:37)
U. "Died" — in this world.
V. "By the plague" — in the world to come.

What about counterparts in Israel, from the Torah forward? The issue concerns the Generation of the Wilderness, which rejected the Land; the party of Korah; and the Ten Tribes. These match the gentile contingents. But here there is a dispute, and no normative judgment emerges from the Mishnah's treatment of the matter:

MISHNAH-TRACTATE SANHEDRIN 11:4

A. "The generation of the wilderness has no portion in the world to come and will not stand in judgment,
B. "for it is written, 'In this wilderness they shall be consumed and there they shall die' (Num. 14:35), "The words of R. Aqiba.
C. R. Eliezer says, "Concerning them it says, 'Gather my saints together to me, those that have made a covenant with me by sacrifice' (Ps. 50:5)."
D. "The party of Korah is not destined to rise up,
E. "for it is written, 'And the earth closed upon them' — in this world.
F. "'And they perished from among the assembly' — in the world to come," the words of R. Aqiba.
G. And R. Eliezer says, "Concerning them it says, 'The Lord kills and resurrects, brings down to Sheol and brings up again' (1 Sam. 2:6)."

MISHNAH-TRACTATE SANHEDRIN 11:5

A. "The ten tribes [of northern Israel, exiled by the Assyrians] are not destined to return [with Israel at the time of the resurrection of the dead],
B. "since it is said, 'And he cast them into another land, as on this day' (Deut. 29:28). Just as the day passes and does not return, so they have gone their way and will not return," the words of R. Aqiba.
C. R. Eliezer says, "Just as this day is dark and then grows light, so the ten tribes for whom it now is dark — thus in the future it is destined to grow light for them."

Scripture thus contributes the details that refine the basic proposition; the framer has found the appropriate exclusions. But the prophet, in Scripture, also has provided the basic allegation on which all else rests, that is, "Israel will be entirely righteous and inherit the land forever." Denying the stated dogmas removes a person from the status of "Israel," in line with the opening statement, so to be Israel means to rise from the dead, and Israel as a collectivity is defined as those persons in humanity who are destined to eternal life, a supernatural community. So much for the initial statement of the eschatological doctrine in the Talmud.

v. How the Talmud Finds in Scripture the Foundations for the Doctrine of Resurrection.. Bavli Sanhedrin 11:1 I.27ff./91bff

Among the components of that doctrine, that resurrection of the dead is a doctrine set forth by Scripture and demonstrable within the framework of the Torah occupies a principal place in the Talmud's exposition of the topic. Our outline of the chapter has already shown the context in which the demonstration takes place, the justification of denial of resurrection to those that deny the Torah makes that promise. Now the affirmative case is made.

Bavli Sanhedrin 11:1/I.2-14/90b-91b

I.2 A. How, on the basis of the Torah, do we know about the resurrection of the dead?
  B. As it is said, "And you shall give thereof the Lord's heave-offering to Aaron the priest" (Num. 18:28).
  C. And will Aaron live forever? And is it not the case that he did not even get to enter the Land of Israel, from the produce of which heave-offering is given? [So there is no point in Aaron's life at which he would receive the priestly rations.]
  D. Rather, this teaches that he is destined once more to live, and the Israelites will give him heave-offering.
  E. On the basis of this verse, therefore, we see that the resurrection of the dead is a teaching of the Torah.

Now come the patriarchs, who also will rise from the dead:

I.4 A. It has been taught on Tannaite authority:
  B. R. Simai says, "How on the basis of the Torah do we know about the resurrection of the dead?
  C. "As it is said, 'And I also have established my covenant with [the patriarchs] to give them the land of Canaan' (Ex. 6:4).
  D. "'With you' is not stated, but rather, 'with them,' indicating on the basis of the Torah that there is the resurrection of the dead."

The question is then re-framed, no longer in terms of proof based on the facts of Scripture, but now in more general terms. Sectarians ask how we know that God will do this thing:

I.5 A. Minim asked Rabban Gamaliel, "How do we know that the Holy One, blessed be he, will resurrect the dead?"

Proofs from Scripture will not serve when dealing with outsiders to the community of the Torah:

B. He said to them, "It is proved from the Torah, from the Prophets, and from the Writings." But they did not accept his proofs.

In each of the three matched demonstrations, a verse is adduced but interpreted in some way other than the proposed one:

C. "From the Torah: for it is written, 'And the Lord said to Moses, Behold, you shall sleep with your fathers and rise up' (Deut. 31:16)."
D. They said to him, "But perhaps the sense of the passage is, 'And the people will rise up' (Deut. 31:16)?"
E. "From the Prophets: as it is written, 'Thy dead men shall live, together with my dead body they shall arise. Awake and sing, you that live in the dust, for your dew is as the dew of herbs, and the earth shall cast out its dead' (Is. 26:19)."
F. "But perhaps that refers to the dead whom Ezekiel raised up."
G. "From the Writings, as it is written, 'And the roof of your mouth, like the best wine of my beloved, that goes down sweetly, causing the lips of those who are asleep to speak' (Song 7:9)."
H. "But perhaps this means that the dead will move their lips?"
I. That would accord with the view of R. Yohanan.
J. For R. Yohanan said in the name of R. Simeon b. Yehosedeq, "Any authority in whose name a law is stated in this world moves his lips in the grave,
K. "as it is said, 'Causing the lips of those that are asleep to speak.'"

Finally, Gamaliel is able to find a pertinent verse that the sectarians could accept; why this proof served and the prior ones did not would yield insight into sages' characterization of their critics:

L. [The minim would not concur in Gamaliel's view] until he cited for them the following verse: "'Which the Lord swore to your fathers to give to them' (Deut. 11:21) — to them and not to you, so proving from the Torah that the dead will live."
M. And there are those who say that it was the following verse that he cited to them: "'But you who cleaved to the Lord you God are alive, everyone of you this day' (Deut. 4:4). Just as on this day all of you are alive, so in the world to come all of you will live."

The successful proof involves little more than a dismissal of the others, at L, or a reaffirmation of the faith — Israel cleaves to the Lord — at M.

From the sectarians, we take a step still further outside the circle of faith and deal with "Romans" (which in some MSS becomes Aramaeans). Now the discussion is broadened to God's knowledge of the future as well as his power to raise the dead:

5. The Talmud's Union of Halakhah and Aggadah...

I.6   A.   Romans asked R. Joshua b. Hananiah, "How do we know that the Holy One will bring the dead to life and also that he knows what is going to happen in the future?"
      B.   He said to them, "Both propositions derive from the following verse of Scripture:
      C.   "As it is said, 'And the Lord said to Moses, Behold you shall sleep with you fathers and rise up again, and this people shall go awhoring ...' (Deut. 31:16)."
      D.   "But perhaps the sense is, '[the people] will rise up and go awhoring'
      E.   He said to them, "Then you have gained half of the matter, that God knows what is going to happen in the future."

Another composition goes over the same matter, now not with sectarians in view:

I.7   A.   It has also been stated on Amoraic authority:
      B.   Said R. Yohanan in the name of R. Simeon b. Yohai, "How do we know that the Holy One, blessed be he, will bring the dead to life and knows what is going to happen in the future?
      C.   "As it is said, 'Behold, you shall sleep with you fathers, and ... rise again ... (Deut. 31:16)."

The sectarians now deny that the Torah teaches the principle of resurrection:

I.8   A.   It has been taught on Tannaite authority:
      B.   Said R. Eliezer b. R. Yosé, "In this matter I proved false the books of the minim.
      C.   "For they would say, 'The principle of the resurrection of the dead does not derive from the Torah.'
      D.   "I said to them, 'You have forged your Torah and have gained nothing on that account.
      E.   "'For you say, "The principle of the resurrection of the dead does not derive from the Torah."
      F.   "'Lo, Scripture says, "[Because he has despised the Lord of the Lord ...] that soul shall be cut off completely, his iniquity shall be upon him" (Num. 15:31).
      G.   "' "... shall be utterly cut off ...," in this world, in which case, at what point will "... his iniquity be upon him ..."?
      H.   "'Will it not be in the world to come?'"
      I.   Said R. Pappa to Abbayye, "And might one not have replied to them that the words 'utterly ...' '... cut off ...,' signify the two worlds [this and the next]?"
      J.   [He said to him,] "They would have answered, 'The Torah speaks in human language [and the doubling of the verb carries no meaning beyond its normal sense].'"

Sages pursue the same dispute:

I.9 A. This accords with the following Tannaite dispute:
B. "'That soul shall be utterly cut off' — 'shall be cut off' — in this world, 'utterly' — in the world to come," the words of R. Aqiba.
C. Said R. Ishmael to him, "And has it not been said, 'He reproaches the Lord, and that soul shall be cut off' (Num. 15:31). Does this mean that there are three worlds?
D. "Rather: '... it will be cut off ...,' in this world, '... utterly ...,' in the world to come, and 'utterly cut off ...,' indicates that the Torah speaks in ordinary human language."

Subsidiary questions now arise: what will the dead be wearing?

I.10 A. Queen Cleopatra asked R. Meir, saying, "I know that the dead will live, for it is written, 'And [the righteous] shall blossom forth out of your city like the grass of the earth' (Ps. 72:16).
B. "But when they rise, will they rise naked or in their clothing?"
C. He said to her, "It is an argument a fortiori based on the grain of wheat.
D. "Now if a grain of wheat, which is buried naked, comes forth in many garments, the righteous, who are buried in their garments, all the more so [will rise in many garments]!"

From one royal figure we move on to another, and the colloquy leaves the framework of Scripture's facts and proceeds to arguments built on analogies drawn from nature. How can the dead be reconstituted out of the dirt?

I.11 A. Caesar said to Rabban Gamaliel, "You maintain that the dead will live. But they are dust, and can the dust live?"
B. [91A] His daughter said to him, "Allow me to answer him:
C. "There are two potters in our town, one who works with water, the other who works with clay. Which is the more impressive?"
D. He said to her, "The one who works with water."
E. She said to him, "If he works with water, will he not create even more out of clay?"

Yet another argument based on analogy is set forth:

I.12 A. A Tannaite authority of the house of R. Ishmael [taught], "[Resurrection] is a matter of an argument a fortiori based on the case of a glass utensil.
B. "Now if glassware, which is the work of the breath of a mortal man, when broken, can be repaired,

5. The Talmud's Union of Halakhah and Aggadah...

C. "A mortal man, who is made by the breath of the Holy One, blessed be he, how much the more so [that he can be repaired, in the resurrection of the dead]."

Dealing with a sectarian, a sage appeals to yet another analogy, now in the narrative form of a parable:

I.13 A. A min said to R. Ammi, "You say that the dead will live. But they are dust, and will the dust live?"
B. He said to him, "I shall draw a parable for you. To what may the matter be compared?
C. "It may be compared to the case of a mortal king, who said to his staff, 'Go and build a great palace for me, in a place in which there is no water or dirt [for bricks].
D. "They went and built it, but after a while it collapsed.
E. "He said to them, 'Go and rebuild it in a place in which there are dirt and water [for bricks].'
F. "They said to him, 'We cannot do so.'
G. "He became angry with them and said to them, 'In a place in which there is neither water nor dirt you were able to build, and now in a place in which there are water and dirt, how much the more so [should you be able to build it]!'
H. "And if you [the min] do not believe it, go to a valley and look at a rat, which today is half-flesh and half-dirt and tomorrow will turn into a creeping thing, made all of flesh. Will you say that it takes much time? Then go up to a mountain and see that today there is only one snail, but tomorrow it will rain and the whole of it will be filled with snails."

Further proofs from Scripture that the dead will be resurrected include the following systematic statements.

In this protracted demonstration, certainly the Bavli's single most ambitious composite, the first proof appeals to the formulation of Scripture, its language bearing the implication that Moses and the children of Israel who sang the song at the sea will rise from the dead:

BAVLI SANHEDRIN 11:1 I.27FF./91BFF

I.27 A. It has been taught on Tannaite authority:
B. R. Meir says, "How on the basis of the Torah do we know about the resurrection of the dead?
C. "As it is said, 'Then shall Moses and the children of Israel sing this song to the Lord' (Ex. 15:1).
D. "What is said is not 'sang' but 'will sing,' on the basis of which there is proof from the Torah of the resurrection of the dead.
E. "Along these same lines: 'Then shall Joshua build an altar to the Lord God of Israel' (Josh. 8:30).

F. "What is said is not 'built' but 'will build,' on the basis of which there is proof from the Torah of the resurrection of the dead.
G. Then what about this verse: "Then will Solomon build a high place for Chemosh, abomination of Moab" (1 Kgs.. 11:7)? Does it mean that he will build it? Rather, Scripture treats him as though he had built it [even though he had merely thought about doing so].

From proof of that kind, numerous extensions emerge, all of them appealing to the use of the future tense:

I.28 A. Said R. Joshua b. Levi, "How on the basis of Scripture may we prove the resurrection of the dead?
B. "As it is said, 'Blessed are those who dwell in your house, they shall ever praise you, selah' (Ps. 84:5).
C. "What is said is not 'praised you' but 'shall praise you,' on the basis of which there is proof from the Torah of the resurrection of the dead."
D. And R. Joshua b. Levi said, "Whoever recites the song [of praise] in this world will have the merit of saying it in the world to come,
E. "as it is said, 'Happy are those who dwell in you house, they shall ever praise you, selah' (Ps. 84:5)."

The same kind of proof follows:

F. Said R. Hiyya b. Abba said R. Yohanan, "On what basis do we know about the resurrection of the dead from Scripture."
G. "As it says, 'Your watchman shall lift up the voice, with the voice together they shall sing (Is. 52:8).'"
H. What is said is not 'sang' but 'will sing' on the basis of which there is proof from the Torah of the resurrection of the dead.
I. Said R. Yohanan, "In the future all the prophets will sing in unison, as it is written, 'Your watchman shall lift up the voice, with the voice together they shall sing (Is. 57:8).'"

Now we turn to individuals and how they are represented in Scripture. Here that Reuben will live bears the implication of resurrection, since we know he died:

I.31 A. Said Raba, "How on the basis of the Torah do we find evidence for the resurrection of the dead?
B. "As it is said, 'Let Reuben live and not die' (Deut. 33:6).
C. "'Let Reuben live' in this world, and 'not die', in the world to come."

5. The Talmud's Union of Halakhah and Aggadah...

The book of Daniel contains more explicit evidence:

D. Rabina said, "Proof derives from here: 'And many of them that sleep in the dust of the earth shall awake, some to everlasting life, and some to shame and everlasting contempt.' (Dan. 12:2)."

E. R. Ashi said, "Proof derives from here: 'But go your way till the end be, for you shall rest and stand in your lot at the end of days' (Dan. 12:13)."

Wisdom-literature likewise serves, an analogy deriving from a statement in Proverbs:

I.33 A. Said R. Tabi said R. Josiah, "What is the meaning of this verse of Scripture: 'The grave and the barren womb and the earth that is not filled by water' (Prov. 30:16).

B. "What has the grave to do with the womb?

C. "It is to say to you, just as the womb takes in and gives forth, so Sheol takes in and gives forth.

D. "And is it not an argument a fortiori? If in the case of the womb, in which they insert [something] in secret, the womb brings forth in loud cries, Sheol, into which [bodies] are placed with loud cries, is it not reasonable to suppose that from the grave people will be brought forth with great cries?

E. "On the basis of this argument there is an answer to those who say that the doctrine of the resurrection of the dead does not derive from the Torah."

The final proof of interest here concerns the fate of those who are resurrected. When they are restored to life, it is in a condition of perfection, so they will never (again) die, an important point for a restorationist theology:

I.34 A. A Tannaite authority of the house of Elisha [taught], "The righteous whom the Holy One, blessed be he, is going to resurrect will not revert to dust,

B. "for it is said, 'And it shall come to pass that he that is left in Zion and he that remains in Jerusalem shall be called holy, even everyone that is written among the living in Jerusalem, (Is. 4:3).

C. "Just as the Holy One lives forever, so they shall live forever.

D. [92B] "And if you want to ask, as to those years in which the Holy One, blessed be he, will renew his world, as it is said, 'And the Lord alone shall be exalted in that day' (Is. 2:11), during that time what will the righteous do?

E. "The answer is that the Holy One, blessed be he, will make them wings like eagles, and they will flutter above the water, as it is said, 'Therefore will not fear, when the earth be moved and the mountains be carried in the midst of the sea' (Ps. 44:3).

F. "And if you should say that they will have pain [in all this], Scripture says, 'But those who wait upon the Lord shall renew their strength, they shall mount up with wings as eagles, they shall run and not be weary, they shall walk and not be faint' (Is. 40:31)."

The details of judgment that follows resurrection prove less ample. The basic account stresses that God will judge with great mercy. But the Talmud presents no fully-articulated story of judgment. Even the detail that through repentance and death man has already atoned, which is stated in so many words in the context of repentance and atonement, plays no role that I can discern in discussions of the last judgment.

VI. The Outcome of the Union of Halakhah and Aggadah

The main point yielded by the union of the Halakhah and the Aggadah in Bavli-tractate Sanhedrin registers cannot be missed. The death penalty guarantees the criminal or sinner a portion in the world to come. Capital punishment brings about atonement for gross sin that leaves the sinner or criminal free of further guilt. The Halakhah explicitly states that the death penalty guarantees the sinner or criminal a place in the Garden of Eden when it asks, what shall we make of the Israelite sinner or criminal? Specifically, does the sin or crime, which has estranged him from God, close the door to life eternal? If it does, then justice is implacable and perfect. If it does not, then God shows his mercy — but what of justice?

We can understand the Halakhic answer only if we keep in mind that the Halakhah takes for granted the Aggadic narrative concerning resurrection of the dead, the final judgment, and the life of the world to come beyond the grave: "All Israelites have a portion in the world to come," with exclusions not encompassing those put to death for mortal sin or crime. From that perspective, death becomes an event in life but not the end of life. And, it must follow, the death penalty too does not mark the utter annihilation of the person of the sinner or criminal. On the contrary, because the criminal or sinner pays for his crime or sin in this life, he situates himself with all of the rest of supernatural Israel, ready for the final judgment. Having been judged, he will "stand in judgment," meaning, he will be found ultimately justified and worthy of the life of the world to come along with everyone else. So punishment takes place now, eternal life later on.

Accordingly, given their theological-Aggadic conviction, inexorable within monotheism, that all Israel possesses a share in the world to come, meaning, nearly everybody will rise from the grave, the sages took as their Halakhic task the specification of how, in this world, criminals-sinners would receive appropriate punishment in a proper procedure, so that, in the world to come, they would take their place along with everyone else in the resurrection and eternal life. The Talmud's union of Halakhah and Aggadah finally resolves monotheism's dilemma: how, given the condition of humanity, is God both all-powerful and just? Without the answer, "wait and see," all is lost. The theology narrated in the Aggadah and realized in the Halakhah defines the human condition: it is to hope. For an Israelite, it is a sin to despair. That is not a mere sentiment, it is an explicit judgment of the Talmud on the outcome of the Torah: what captures the whole all together and all at once.

ENDNOTES

[1] Zoroastrianism, Christianity, and Islam set forth the same narrative of reward and punishment.
[2] The Talmud places the chapter beginning "All Israelites have a share in the world to come" at the end, as Chapter Eleven. The Mishnah places it as Chapter Ten, and the Talmud's Chapter Ten is the Mishnah's Chapter Eleven. I follow the order of the Talmud throughout.
[3] As noted, the Bavli numbers this chapter as eleven, the Mishnah places it as ten.

6

Epilogue

Defining Judaism

The Other Side of Reason: Let God be God

The Talmud defined the religion that the world knows as Judaism. This it did in two ways. First, it systematized and organized details into a coherent, rational structure. Second, it left open the space for God to be God, beyond all system and rationality. The system and the order come first, then the Talmud's confession of the open-ended mystery of God completes the narrative.

I. Defining Judaism, Explaining History.
Bavli Makkot 3:15-16 II.1/23b-24a, Bavli Makkot 3:15-16 II.4/24a-b

Here is how the way of life of the Halakhah is recapitulated and reconstructed by the Aggadah. In the very context of history that way of life is shown to be rational and subject to reliable rules, the whole meant to realize God's plan for humanity.

Bavli Makkot 3:15-16 II.1/23b-24a

A. R. Hananiah b. Aqashia says, "The Holy One, blessed be he, wanted to give merit to Israel.
B. "Therefore he gave them abundant Torah and numerous commandments,
C. "as it is said, 'It pleased the Lord for his righteousness' sake to magnify the Torah and give honor to it (Is. 42:21)."

Mishnah-tractate Makkot 3:16

II.1. A. **Therefore he gave them abundant Torah and numerous commandments:**

B. R. Simelai expounded, "Six hundred and thirteen commandments were given to Moses, three hundred and sixty-five negative ones, corresponding to the number of the days of the solar year, and two hundred forty-eight positive commandments, corresponding to the parts of man's body."

C. Said R. Hamnuna, *"What verse of Scripture indicates that fact?* 'Moses commanded us Torah, an inheritance of the congregation of Jacob' (Dt. 33:4). *The numerical value assigned to the letters of the word Torah is* **[24A]** *six hundred and eleven, not counting,* 'I am' and 'you shall have no other gods,' *since these have come to us from the mouth of the Almighty."*

D. [Simelai continues:] "David came and reduced them to eleven: 'A Psalm of David: Lord, who shall sojourn in thy tabernacle, and who shall dwell in thy holy mountain? (i) He who walks uprightly and (ii) works righteousness and (iii) speaks truth in his heart and (iv) has no slander on his tongue and (v) does no evil to his fellow and (vi) does not take up a reproach against his neighbor, (vii) in whose eyes a vile person is despised but (viii) honors those who fear the Lord. (ix) He swears to his own hurt and changes not. (x) He does not lend on interest. (xi) He does not take a bribe against the innocent' (Psalm 15)."

E. "He who walks uprightly:" this is Abraham: "Walk before me and be wholehearted" (Gen. 17:1).

F. "and works righteousness:" this is Abba Hilqiahu.

G. "speaks truth in his heart:" for instance R. Safra.

H. "has no slander on his tongue:" this is our father, Jacob: "My father might feel me and I shall seem to him as a deceiver" (Gen. 27:12).

I. "does no evil to his fellow:" he does not go into competition with his fellow craftsman.

J. "does not take up a reproach against his neighbor:" this is someone who befriends his relatives.

K. "in whose eyes a vile person is despised:" this is Hezekiah, king of Judah, who dragged his father's bones on a rope bed.

L. "honors those who fear the Lord:" this is Jehoshaphat, king of Judah, who, whenever he would see a disciple of a sage, would rise from his throne and embrace and kiss him and call him, "My father, my father, my lord, my lord, my master, my master."

M. "He swears to his own hurt and changes not:" this is R. Yohanan.

N. For said R. Yohanan, "I shall continue fasting until I get home."

O. "He does not lend on interest:" not even interest from a gentile.

P. "He does not take a bribe against the innocent:" such as R. Ishmael b. R. Yosé.

Q. "He who does these things shall never be moved:"

6. Epilogue. Defining Judaism

R. When Rabban Gamaliel *reached this verse of Scripture, he would weep, saying, "If someone did all of these [virtuous deeds], then he will never be moved, but not merely on account of one of them."*

S. They said to him, "Is it written, 'Who does all of these things;'? What is written is only 'who does these things,' meaning, even one of them."

T. "For if you do not say this, then there is another verse of Scripture of which we have to take account: 'Do not defile yourselves in all of these things' (Lev. 18:24). Does this mean that one is unclean only if he touches all of these things, but not if he touches only one of them? But does it not mean, only one of them:?

U. "Here too it means that only one of these things is sufficient."

V. [Simelai continues:] "Isaiah came and reduced them to six: '(i) He who walks righteously and (ii) speaks uprightly, (iii) he who despises the gain of oppressions, (iv) shakes his hand from holding bribes, (v) stops his ear from hearing of blood (vi) and shuts his eyes from looking upon evil, he shall dwell on high' (Isaiah 33:25-26)."

W. "He who walks righteously:" this is our father, Abraham: "For I have known him so that he may command his children and his household after him" (Gen. 18:19).

X. "speaks uprightly:" this is one who does not belittle his fellow in public.

Y. "he who despises the gain of oppressions:" for example, R. Ishmael b. Elisha.

Z. "shakes his hand from holding bribes:" for example, R. Ishmael b. R. Yosé.

AA. "stops his ear from hearing of blood:" *who will not listen to demeaning talk about a disciple of rabbis and remain silent.*

BB. *For instance, R. Eleazar b. R. Simeon.*

CC. "and shuts his eyes from looking upon evil:" that is in line with what R. Hiyya bar Abba said.

DD. For said R. Hiyya bar Abba, "This is someone who does not stare at women as they are standing and washing clothes.

EE. Concerning such a man it is written, "he shall dwell on high."

FF. [Simelai continues:] "Micah came and reduced them to three: 'It has been told you, man, what is good, and what the Lord demands from you, (i) only to do justly and (ii) to love mercy, and (iii) to walk humbly before God' (Micah 6:8)."

GG. "only to do justly:" this refers to justice.

HH. "to love mercy:" this refers to doing acts of loving kindness.

II. "to walk humbly before God:" this refers to accompanying a corpse to the grave and welcoming the bread.

JJ. And does this not yield a conclusion a fortiori: if matters that are not ordinarily done in private are referred to by the Torah as "walking humbly before God," all the more so matters that ordinarily are done in private.

KK. [Simelai continues:] "Isaiah again came and reduced them to two : 'Thus says the Lord, (i) Keep justice and (ii) do righteousness' (Isaiah 56:1).
LL. "Amos came and reduced them to a single one, as it is said, 'For thus says the Lord to the house of Israel. Seek Me and live.'"
MM. Objected R. Nahman bar Isaac, "Maybe the sense is, 'seek me' through the whole of the Torah?"
NN. Rather, [Simelai continues:] "Habakkuk further came and based them on one, as it is said, 'But the righteous shall live by his faith' (Habakkuk 2:4)."

The same passage continues with a succinct description of the pattern of history and how Israel will be redeemed. Here is the counterpart to Simelai's systematization of the religious duties into a single encompassing statement: all the duties serve to realize the imperative of living by trust in God. Now the same imperative is illustrated in the concrete situation of Israel awaiting redemption.

BAVLI MAKKOT 3:15-16 II.4/24A-B

II.4.A. Once upon a time Rabban Gamaliel, R. Eleazar b. Azariah, R. Joshua, and R. Aqiba were walking along the way and heard the roar of Rome all the way from Puteoli, at a distance of a hundred and twenty miles. They began to cry, but R. Aqiba brightened up.
B. They said to him, "Why so cheerful?"
C. He said to them, "Why so gloomy?"
D. They said to him, "These 'Cushites' worship sticks and stones and burn incense to idolatry but live in safety and comfort, while as to us, the house that was the footstool for our God is burned [24B] with fire! Why shouldn't we cry?!"
E. He said to them, "But that's precisely why I rejoice. If those who violate his will have it so good, those who do his will all the more so!"

II.5.A. Once again, they were going up to Jerusalem. When they got to Mount Scopus, they tore their garments. When they reached the Temple mount, they saw a fox emerge from the house of the Holy of Holies. They began to cry, but R. Aqiba brightened up.
B. They said to him, "Why so cheerful?"
C. He said to them, "Why so gloomy?"
D. They said to him, "The place of which it once was said, 'And the non-priest who draws near shall be put to death' (Num. 1:51) has become a fox hole, so shouldn't we weep?"
E. He said to them, "But that's precisely why I rejoice. It is written, 'And I will take to me faithful witnesses to record, Uriah the priest and Zechariah son of Jeberechiah' (Is. 8:2). And what has Uriah the priest to do with Zechariah? Uriah lived during the first Temple, and Zechariah during the second, but Scripture had linked the prophecy of Zechariah to the prophecy of Uriah. In the case of

6. Epilogue. Defining Judaism

Uriah: 'Therefore shall Zion for your sake be ploughed as a field' (Mic. 3:12). Zechariah: 'Thus says the Lord of hosts, there shall yet old men and old women sit in the broad places of Jerusalem' (Zech. 8:4). Until the prophecy of Uriah was fulfilled, I was afraid that the prophecy of Zechariah might not be fulfilled. Now that the prophecy of Uriah has come about, we may be certain that the prophecy of Zechariah will be fulfilled word for word."

F. They said to him, "Aqiba, you have given us comfort, Aqiba, you have given us comfort."

The comfort derives from the reliability of history: the rules work. But the Talmud encompasses a jarring note, on which we close.

II. LET GOD BE GOD. BAVLI MENAHOT 3:7 II.5/29B

This book has represented the Talmud as a supremely rational, purely intellectual formulation of culture. But we find, buried in its pages, reminders that God is always God: responsive to rules but free to govern by his unfettered will. The mystery of Creation, the message of Revelation, the marvel of Redemption — these acts adumbrate, give signals of, God's being. They do not tell humanity more than what God wants known by humanity. The Talmud's greatness lies in its invitation to humanity to unite society to the sublime, bridge the gap between the here and now and what lies beyond. Reason and criticism — the way from humanity's mind to God's — carry so far as God wills the path to God to lead. In the end, God is always God, humanity remains for eternity the creature of God: like God, but not God.

BAVLI MENAHOT 3:7 II.5/29B

II.5 A. Said R. Judah said Rab, "At the time that Moses went up on high, he found the Holy One in session, affixing crowns to the letters [of the words of the Torah]. He said to him, 'Lord of the universe, who is stopping you [from regarding the document as perfect without these additional crowns on the letters]?'

B. "He said to him, 'There is a man who is going to arrive at the end of many generations, and Aqiba b. Joseph is his name, who is going to interpret on the basis of each point of the crowns heaps and heaps of laws.'

C. "He said to him, 'Lord of the Universe, show him to me.'

D. "He said to him, 'Turn around.'

E. "He went and took a seat at the end of eight rows, but he could not grasp what the people were saying. He felt faint. But when the discourse reached a certain matter, and the disciples said, 'My lord, how do you know this?' and he answered, 'It is a law given to Moses from Sinai,' he regained his composure.

F. "He went and came before the Holy One. He said before him, 'Lord of the Universe, How come you have someone like that and yet you give the Torah through me?'
G. "He said to him, 'Silence! That is how the thought came to me.'
H. "He said to him, 'Lord of the Universe, you have shown me his Torah, now show me his reward.'
I. "He said to him, 'Turn around.'
J. "He turned around and saw his flesh being weighed out at the butcher-stalls in the market.
K. "He said to him, 'Lord of the Universe, 'Such is Torah, such is the reward?'
L. "He said to him, 'Silence! That is how the thought came to me.'"

There abides beyond time and space an intellect and will that even Halakhic reasoning cannot reach, even Aggadic narrative cannot replicate. God consulted the Torah to create the world, but God is God beyond the Torah. The Talmud forms a testament to the humility of humanity, even in the aspect of intellect, in which it takes pride.

For Further Reference

BIBLIOGRAPHY: The best starting point for further study of any topic of Rabbinic Judaism, including the Talmud of Babylonia, is Guenter Stemberger, *Introduction to the Talmud and Midrash*, translated and edited by Markus Bockmuehl. 2nd ed., Edinburgh: T. & T. Clark, 1996.

Note also the compendious bibliography to 1980 on the Talmud of Babylonia by David Goodblatt in J. Neusner, editor, *The Study of Ancient Judaism*. N.Y., 1981: Ktav. Second printing. Atlanta, 1992: Scholars Press for South Florida Studies in the History of Judaism. Now: Lanham MD, 2000: University Press of America. II. *The Study of Ancient Judaism: The Palestinian and Babylonian Talmuds*.

TRANSLATIONS: My translation and commentary to the Mishnah and the Tosefta are as follows: *A History of the Mishnaic Law of Purities*. Leiden, 1974-1977: Brill. I-XXII; *A History of the Mishnaic Law of Holy Things*. Leiden, Brill: 1979. I-VI; *A History of the Mishnaic Law of Women*. Leiden, Brill: 1979-1980. I-V; *A History of the Mishnaic Law of Appointed Times*. Leiden, Brill: 1981-1983. I-V; *A History of the Mishnaic Law of Damages*. Leiden, Brill: 1983-1985. I-V; *The Mishnah. A New Translation*. New Haven and London, 1987: Yale University Press. *Choice* Outstanding Academic Book List, 1989. Second printing: 1990. Paperbound edition: 1991. CD Rom edition: Logos, 1996. CD Rom/Web edition: OakTree Software, Inc. Altamonte Springs, FL.

In addition, I serve as editor of *The Law of Agriculture in the Mishnah and the Tosefta. Translation, commentary, theology*. Leiden, 2005: E. J. Brill. I. *Berakhot*, Translation and commentary by Tzvee Zahavy. Theological Afterword by Jacob Neusner (2004) II. *Peah*. Translation and commentary by Roger Brooks. Theological Afterword by Jacob Neusner III. *Demai*. Translation and commentary by Richard Sarason. Theological afterword by Jacob Neusner IV. *Kilayim*. Translation and commentary by Irving Mandelbaum. Theological afterword by Jacob Neusner V. *Shebiit*. Translation and commentary by Louis Newman. Theological afterword by Jacob Neusner VI. *Terumot*. Translation and commentary by Alan J. Avery-Peck. Theological afterword by Jacob Neusner VII. *Maaserot*. Translation and commentary by Martin Jaffee. Theological afterword by Jacob Neusner VIII. *Maaser Sheni*. Translation and commentary by Peter Haas. Theological afterword by Jacob Neusner IX. *Hallah, Orlah, Bikkurim*. Translation and commentary by Avraham Havivi and Alan J. Avery-Peck (Hallah), Howard Essner (Orlah), and Maggie Moors Wenig, and David Weiner (Bikkurim). Theological afterword by

Jacob Neusner X. *A History of the Mishnaic Law of Agriculture.* By Alan J. Avery-Peck

Note also *The Tosefta. Translated from the Hebrew.* N.Y., 1977-1980: Ktav. II-VI. I. Editor: *The Tosefta. Translated from the Hebrew. I. The First Division Zeraim.* N.Y., 1985: Ktav. II. *The Tosefta. Translated from the Hebrew. The Second Division. Moed.* Second printing: Atlanta, 1999: Scholars Press for USF Academic Commentary Series. III. *The Tosefta. Translated from the Hebrew. The Third Division. Nashim.* Second printing: Atlanta, 1999: Scholars Press for USF Academic Commentary Series. IV. *The Tosefta. Translated from the Hebrew. The Fourth Division. Neziqin.* Second printing: Atlanta, 1999: Scholars Press for USF Academic Commentary Series V. *The Tosefta. Translated from the Hebrew. The Fifth Division. Qodoshim.* Second printing: Atlanta, 1997: Scholars Press for USF Academic Commentary Series VI. *The Tosefta. Translated from the Hebrew. The Sixth Division. Tohorot.* Second printing: Atlanta, 1990: Scholars Press for *South Florida Studies in the History of Judaism.* With a new preface. Reprint: *The Tosefta in English.* I. *Zeraim, Moed, and Nashim.* Peabody, 2003: Hendrickson Publications. With a new introduction. Reprint: *The Tosefta in English.* II. *Neziqin, Qodoshim, and Tohorot.* Peabody, 2003: Hendrickson Publications.

My complete translations, commentaries, outlines, and comparative outlines of both Talmuds, in numerous volumes and parts, are as follows:

The Talmud of Babylonia. An American Translation. Chico, then Atlanta: 1984-1995: Scholars Press for Brown Judaic Studies. Now: Lanham, MD: University Press of America.

The Talmud of Babylonia. An Academic Commentary. Atlanta, 1994-1999: Scholars Press for *USF Academic Commentary Series.* Reprint in twenty-two volumes: Peabody, 2005: Hendrickson Publications.

The Talmud of Babylonia. A Complete Outline. Atlanta, 1995-6: Scholars Press for *USF Academic Commentary Series.* Now: Lanham, MD. University Press of America.

On the Yerushalmi, that of my co-workers and myself is the first and only complete translation into English: *The Talmud of the Land of Israel. A Preliminary Translation and Explanation.* Chicago: The University of Chicago Press: 1982-1993.

My systematic analytical commentary is as follows: *The Talmud of the Land of Israel. An Academic Commentary to the Second, Third, and Fourth Divisions.* Atlanta, 1998-1999: Scholars Press for *USF Academic Commentary Series.* Now: Lanham, MD. University Press of America.

The Talmud of The Land of Israel. An Outline of the Second, Third, and Fourth Divisions. Atlanta, 1995-6: Scholars Press for USF Academic Commentary Series. Now: Lanham, MD. University Press of America.

The Two Talmuds Compared. Atlanta, 1995-6: Scholars Press for USF Academic Commentary Series.

For Further Reference

All of these works are planned for a CD edition by Hendrickson Publishing Company, Peabody, MA.

My translation of the Talmud of Babylonia frequently refers to that published by the Soncino Press, London, from the 1930s forward, *The Babylonian Talmud*, and presented in a complete edition in eighteen volumes in 1948, with an index published in 1952. The Hebrew-English edition, with the Hebrew-Aramaic text and English translation on facing pages, is as follows:

Hebrew-English edition of the Babylonian Talmud, under the editorship of I. Epstein. London: Soncino, 1960-.

The Soncino translation, accomplished in a difficult period before and during World War II, invented the English needed for the Gemara, just as Herbert Danby, in his translation of the Mishnah somewhat earlier, had created an English language suitable for the Rabbinic law. Danby and the Soncino group not only pioneered, for the English language, in the presentation of Rabbinic literature; but they accomplished work as enduring in its value and interest as they could have hoped. I have not improved on their word-choices in any way. My contribution is to signal the traits of the document and the logic of its composition and agglutination, to differentiate long columns of type into thought-units and to show their relationships to the continuing discourse.

Where in my translation I use the Soncino translator's wording, I include the translator's name in square brackets to give him credit for the formulation; I also cite his notes verbatim and so indicate, including page and note references where needed. I do not believe the Soncino translators ever received the credit that was coming to them for their intellectual achievement, because the work of translation was not understood as on-going and the task was not perceived as one of problem-solving. But they accomplished more, solved more problems, proved more inventive, than many of the scholars who dismissed their work as, at best, useful. Their translation formed a commentary to the Bavli, one marked by remarkable lucidity of perspective and cogency of comprehension. It is not too much to compare their work to that of Rashi. And no translation into English after theirs did more than improve in detail. All of them, mine included, concur on most questions of meaning, differing in wording and in matters of detail, and then insubstantially.

I translate the standard printed text, universally accessible. For individual tractates we have critical texts, by which people ordinarily mean, collations of variant readings and the like. These are of interest but commonly do not affect the cultural questions of coherence and meaning that occupy us.

OTHER TRANSLATIONS: two current series usefully present the classical text and provide phrase-by-phrase commentaries:

The Artscroll edition: *Bavli. the Gemara: the classic Vilna edition with an annotated interpretive elucidation under the general editorship of* Hersh Goldwurm. *Schottenstein student edition.* New York, 1996: Mesorah Publications.

This is now complete and is the best translation of the Talmud in the classical context.

The Steinsaltz edition: *The Talmud: the Steinsaltz edition, commentary by* Adin Steinsaltz. New York, 1989-: Random House. In this connection note also my *How Adin Steinsaltz Misrepresents the Talmud. Four False Propositions from his "Reference Guide."* Atlanta, 1998: Scholars Press for South Florida Studies in the History of Judaism. Now: Lanham, MD: University Press of America.

Both run into numerous volumes, with introductions and elaborate commentaries, in English translation.

In addition there is the following: A. Ehrman, *The Talmud with English translation and commentary*. Jerusalem, 1965-: El-'Am.

THE TALMUD IN THE CONTEXT OF JUDAISM: My *Judaism. An Introduction.* London and New York, 2002: Penguin provides an account of Judaism, its history, practices, and contemporary expressions.

STUDIES IN JUDAISM
TITLES IN THE SERIES
PUBLISHED BY UNIVERSITY PRESS OF AMERICA

Judith Z. Abrams
The Babylonian Talmud: A Topical Guide, 2002.

Roger David Aus
Matthew 1-2 and the Virginal Conception: In Light of Palestinian and Hellenistic Judaic Traditions on the Birth of Israel's First Redeemer, Moses, 2004.

My Name Is "Legion": Palestinian Judaic Traditions in Mark 5:1-20 and Other Gospel Texts, 2003.

Alan L. Berger, Harry James Cargas, and Susan E. Nowak
The Continuing Agony: From the Carmelite Convent to the Crosses at Auschwitz, 2004.

S. Daniel Breslauer
Creating a Judaism without Religion: A Postmodern Jewish Possibility, 2001.

Bruce Chilton
Targumic Approaches to the Gospels: Essays in the Mutual Definition of Judaism and Christianity, 1986.

David Ellenson
Tradition in Transition: Orthodoxy, Halakhah, and the Boundaries of Modern Jewish Identity, 1989.

Paul V. M. Flesher
New Perspectives on Ancient Judaism, Volume 5: Society and Literature in Analysis, 1990.

Marvin Fox
Collected Essays on Philosophy and on Judaism, Volume One: Greek Philosophy, Maimonides, 2003.

Collected Essays on Philosophy and on Judaism, Volume Two: Some Philosophers, 2003.

Collected Essays on Philosophy and on Judaism, Volume Three: Ethics, Reflections, 2003.

Zev Garber
Methodology in the Academic Teaching of Judaism, 1986.

Zev Garber, Alan L. Berger, and Richard Libowitz
Methodology in the Academic Teaching of the Holocaust, 1988.

Abraham Gross
Spirituality and Law: Courting Martyrdom in Christianity and Judaism, 2005.

Harold S. Himmelfarb and Sergio DellaPergola
Jewish Education Worldwide: Cross-Cultural Perspectives, 1989.

William Kluback
The Idea of Humanity: Hermann Cohen's Legacy to Philosophy and Theology, 1987.

Samuel Morell
Studies in the Judicial Methodology of Rabbi David ibn Abi Zimra, 2004.

Jacob Neusner
Ancient Israel, Judaism, and Christianity in Contemporary Perspective, 2006.

The Aggadic Role in Halakhic Discourses: Volume I, 2001.

The Aggadic Role in Halakhic Discourses: Volume II, 2001.

The Aggadic Role in Halakhic Discourses: Volume III, 2001.

Analysis and Argumentation in Rabbinic Judaism, 2003.

Analytical Templates of the Bavli, 2006.

Ancient Judaism and Modern Category-Formation: "Judaism," "Midrash," "Messianism," and Canon in the Past Quarter Century, 1986.

Canon and Connection: Intertextuality in Judaism, 1987.

Chapters in the Formative History of Judaism. 2006

Dual Discourse, Single Judaism, 2001.

The Emergence of Judaism: Jewish Religion in Response to the Critical Issues of the First Six Centuries, 2000.

First Principles of Systemic Analysis: The Case of Judaism within the History of Religion, 1988.

The Halakhah and the Aggadah, 2001.

Halakhic Hermeneutics, 2003.

Halakhic Theology: A Sourcebook, 2006.

The Hermeneutics of Rabbinic Category Formations, 2001.

How Important Was the Destruction of the Second Temple in the Formation of Rabbinic Judaism? 2006.

How Not to Study Judaism, Examples and Counter-Examples, Volume One: Parables, Rabbinic Narratives, Rabbis' Biographies, Rabbis' Disputes, 2004.

How Not to Study Judaism, Examples and Counter-Examples, Volume Two: Ethnicity and Identity versus Culture and Religion, How Not to Write a Book on Judaism, Point and Counterpoint, 2004.

How the Halakhah Unfolds: Moed Qatan in the Mishnah, ToseftaYerushalmi and Bavli, 2006.

The Implicit Norms of Rabbinic Judaism. 2006.

Intellectual Templates of the Law of Judaism, 2006.

Is Scripture the Origin of the Halakhah? 2005.

Israel and Iran in Talmudic Times: A Political History, 1986.

Israel's Politics in Sasanian Iran: Self-Government in Talmudic Times, 1986.

Judaism in Monologue and Dialogue, 2005.

Major Trends in Formative Judaism, Fourth Series, 2002.

Major Trends in Formative Judaism, Fifth Series, 2002.

Messiah in Context: Israel's History and Destiny in Formative Judaism, 1988.

The Native Category - Formations of the Aggadah: The Later Midrash-Compilations - Volume I, 2000.

The Native Category - Formations of the Aggadah: The Earlier Midrash-Compilations - Volume II, 2000.

Paradigms in Passage: Patterns of Change in the Contemporary Study of Judaism, 1988.

Parsing the Torah, 2005.

Praxis and Parable: The Divergent Discourses of Rabbinic Judaism, 2006.

The Religious Study of Judaism: Description, Analysis and Interpretation, Volume 1, 1986.

The Religious Study of Judaism: Description, Analysis, Interpretation, Volume 2, 1986.

The Religious Study of Judaism: Context, Text, Circumstance, Volume 3, 1987.

The Religious Study of Judaism: Description, Analysis, Interpretation, Volume 4: Ideas of History, Ethics, Ontology, and Religion in Formative Judaism, 1988.

Struggle for the Jewish Mind: Debates and Disputes on Judaism Then and Now, 1988.

The Talmud Law, Theology, Narrative: A Sourcebook, 2005.

Talmud Torah: Ways to God's Presence through Learning: An Exercise in Practical Theology, 2002.

Texts Without Boundaries: Protocols of Non-Documentary Writing in the Rabbinic Canon: Volume I: The Mishnah, Tractate Abot, and the Tosefta, 2002.

Texts Without Boundaries: Protocols of Non-Documentary Writing in the Rabbinic Canon: Volume II: Sifra and Sifré to Numbers, 2002.

Texts Without Boundaries: Protocols of Non-Documentary Writing in the Rabbinic Canon: Volume III: Sifré to Deuteronomy and Mekhilta Attributed to Rabbi Ishmael, 2002.

Texts Without Boundaries: Protocols of Non-Documentary Writing in the Rabbinic Canon: Volume IV: Leviticus Rabbah, 2002.

A Theological Commentary to the Midrash - Volume I: Pesiqta deRab Kahana, 2001.

A Theological Commentary to the Midrash - Volume II: Genesis Raba, 2001.

A Theological Commentary to the Midrash - Volume III: Song of Songs Rabbah, 2001.

A Theological Commentary to the Midrash - Volume IV: Leviticus Rabbah, 2001.

A Theological Commentary to the Midrash - Volume V: Lamentations Rabbati, 2001.

A Theological Commentary to the Midrash - Volume VI: Ruth Rabbah and Esther Rabbah, 2001.

A Theological Commentary to the Midrash - Volume VII: Sifra, 2001.

A Theological Commentary to the Midrash - Volume VIII: Sifré to Numbers and Sifré to Deuteronomy, 2001.

A Theological Commentary to the Midrash - Volume IX: Mekhilta Attributed to Rabbi Ishmael, 2001.

Theological Dictionary of Rabbinic Judaism: Part One: Principal Theological Categories, 2005.

Theological Dictionary of Rabbinic Judaism: Part Two: Making Connections and Building Constructions, 2005.

Theological Dictionary of Rabbinic Judaism: Part Three: Models of Analysis, Explanation, and Anticipation, 2005.

The Theological Foundations of Rabbinic Midrash, 2006.

Theology of Normative Judaism: A Source Book, 2005.

Theology in Action: How the Rabbis of the Talmud Present Theology (Aggadah) in the Medium of the Law (Halakhah). An Anthology, 2006

The Torah and the Halakhah: The Four Relationships, 2003.

The Unity of Rabbinic Discourse: Volume I: Aggadah in the Halakhah, 2001.

The Unity of Rabbinic Discourse: Volume II: Halakhah in the Aggadah, 2001.

The Unity of Rabbinic Discourse: Volume III: Halakhah and Aggadah in Concert, 2001.

The Vitality of Rabbinic Imagination: The Mishnah Against the Bible and Qumran, 2005.

Who, Where and What is "Israel?": Zionist Perspectives on Israeli and American Judaism, 1989.

The Wonder-Working Lawyers of Talmudic Babylonia: The Theory and Practice of Judaism in its Formative Age, 1987.

Jacob Neusner and Ernest S. Frerichs
New Perspectives on Ancient Judaism, Volume 2: Judaic and Christian Interpretation of Texts: Contents and Contexts, 1987.

New Perspectives on Ancient Judaism, Volume 3: Judaic and Christian Interpretation of Texts: Contents and Contexts, 1987.

Jacob Neusner and James F. Strange
Religious Texts and Material Contexts, 2001.

David Novak and Norbert M. Samuelson
Creation and the End of Days: Judaism and Scientific Cosmology, 1986.

Proceedings of the Academy for Jewish Philosophy, 1990.

Aaron D. Panken
The Rhetoric of Innovation: Self-Conscious Legal Change in Rabbinic Literature, 2005.

Norbert M. Samuelson
Studies in Jewish Philosophy: Collected Essays of the Academy for Jewish Philosophy, 1980-1985, 1987.

Benjamin Edidin Scolnic
Alcimus, Enemy of the Maccabees, 2004.

If the Egyptians Drowned in the Red Sea Where are Pharaoh's Chariots?: Exploring the Historical Dimension of the Bible, 2005.

Rivka Ulmer
Pesiqta Rabbati: A Synoptic Edition of Pesiqta Rabbati Based upon all Extant Manuscripts and the Editio Princeps, Volume III, 2002.

Manfred H. Vogel
A Quest for a Theology of Judaism: The Divine, the Human and the Ethical Dimensions in the Structure-of-Faith of Judaism Essays in Constructive, 1987.

Anita Weiner
Renewal: Reconnecting Soviet Jewry to the Soviet People: A Decade of American Jewish Joint Distribution Committee (AJJDC) Activities in the Former Soviet Union 1988-1998, 2003.

Eugene Weiner and Anita Weiner
Israel-A Precarious Sanctuary: War, Death and the Jewish People, 1989.

The Martyr's Conviction: A Sociological Analysis, 2002.

Leslie S. Wilson
The Serpent Symbol in the Ancient Near East: Nahash and Asherah: Death, Life, and Healing, 2001.

www.ingramcontent.com/pod-product-compliance
Lightning Source LLC
Chambersburg PA
CBHW021127300426
44113CB00006B/328